THE HEAD SPEAKS

CHALLENGES AND VISIONS IN EDUCATION

Edited by

Julian Lovelock

Foreword by

Sir Eric Anderson

First published in Great Britain in 2008 by

The University of Buckingham Press

Buckingham MK18 1EG

www.ubpl.co.uk

A CIP catalogue record for this book is available at the British Library

ISBN 10: 0 95546 423 4

ISBN 13: 978 095546 423 2

Cover design by Franks and Franks

For Zoë, Annabel and Edward,

*who, like most Heads' families, too
often took second place to the School.*

Contents

FOREWORD

Sir Eric Anderson

For those tempted to the view that in education we live in the worst of all possible worlds this book is a reminder that the past was not a golden age either. It so happens that His Majesty's Inspectors visited Eton in 1936, the year of publication of *The Head Master Speaks*, one of the parent volumes of this book. Here is an extract from the account of the Science teaching they witnessed:

> The Staff as a whole, with two temporary masters, a number of men filling in odd periods here and there, and one or two members with very slender academic qualifications, does not form a strong and well-balanced team…. All the boys [in their second year], some 200 in number, together with the masters of their Classical Divisions, attend a weekly lecture…. One of the sound lectures was heard; it was illustrated by a wealth of successful experiment, but was far beyond the standard of the boys, and, as far as could be judged, too difficult for the masters who attended to comprehend.

All the original contributors, as quoted in the new volume, confirm that it was not only Eton that had its problems in that area. Their struggle for success is nicely summed up by Roydon Richards of Glasgow Academy, who described himself as "living from one minor crisis to the next" – an experience with which all the modern

i

Heads represented in this volume will be familiar – and complained that "a Head Master's work leaves scanty time for reflecting on fundamental principles".

The contributors to this volume, however, have found time for reflection. I was immediately struck by how similar their concerns are to those of their predecessors, despite all the changes (some for the worse and many for the better) in the seventy-five years which divide them. For instance the Reverend Seniors who spoke in 1936 and the Young Turks of 2008 shake their heads in unison over two over-examined generations. All agree that too many examinations are an incubus and that both parents and governments put too much faith in their results. The Head Master of Ampleforth complained in 1936 that there has never been a "generation so tested", but as the present High Master of Manchester Grammar School points out, we have added since then Key Stage examinations at 7, 11 and 14, as well as hugely increasing the numbers taking GCSE and A level, with central government setting down in ever more prescriptive details what should be taught and how it should be taught. The only consolation comes from the Head Master at Stowe who reports, I am not sure on whose authority, that North Koreans are reputed to be examined even more often than British children.

At least the Reverend Seniors did not have League tables to contend with. The modern Heads think that the malign effect of treating education as a measurable commodity is that the pursuit of grades becomes more important than the acquisition of knowledge or the ability to use it. They also believe (and it is the great feature of the best schools in Britain) that education is not just what happens in the classroom. Important lessons are learned on the games-field, in the theatre and the music department, in debate and competition and all manner of activities out of school hours, and in the shared life of a school which is a community. League tables are so pernicious precisely because the best things in education cannot be measured.

The present generation of Heads has a refreshing view of what education is for. You feel that the government would not understand G. K. Chesterton's description of education as "the soul of society as it passes from one generation to the another", but these Heads do. For them, education is about earning a living but also about "life itself and living life to the full". It is about forming personality, kindling a true love of learning, about inspiration, passion, excellence, excitement, and, as Peter Brodie rightly insists – it should be fun. They do not say it in so many words, but it is obvious that they see their schools as beacons of civilization in a darkly utilitarian world. Their predecessors worried about philistine parents, concerned only that schools should prepare children to earn a living; modern Heads worry more about philistine governments which have meddled endlessly with education, often for social rather than educational reasons.

The one striking difference between 1936 and 2008 is the attitude to religion. 1930's Heads complained that, because society was increasingly irreligious, a proper Christian education was becoming difficult. In modern times School Inspectors talk about the spirituality of the school rather than its religion and, with an ethnic and religious mix undreamed of in the 1930's, schools understandably thrust Christianity to the fore much less. If I read these essays correctly, within schools "Community" has become the new religion.

Respecting and considering the needs of others, tolerance and social responsibility, a community not so much Christian as "based on Christian values" are the aims of the typical good school of today. Now that neither church nor family any longer dictates how the young should think, it is the influence of the school community which shapes the standards by which they live for the greater good.

What would most have astonished the Heads of 1936 is to find the High Masters of Manchester Grammar School and St Paul's having to defend selection. They do so eloquently and persuasively. Ray of Manchester Grammar School deplores the retreat from scholarship. The most able have their own special needs and in 2008 they are the victims of a political anti-selective dogma. There can be no rational justification for saying that ballet dancers, footballers and musicians require to be taught together in groups of like-minded people with the ability in these disciplines but that linguists, engineers and mathematicians should not be so treated.

Stephen, at St Paul's, goes so far as to say that in denying freedom of opportunity to many able British boys and girls the government is infringing their human rights. He suggests re-introducing selection, without the old traumas of the 11+, by allowing all those 14 year-olds who want an academic education to have it – on condition that they are allowed to drop out after a year or whenever they find it is not for them.

That is only one of the many pieces of common sense in these articles. Angela Slater gets to the nub of the problems caused by technology: "searching for information is the easy bit; how to evaluate the information when you have found it is why you need education".

THE HEAD SPEAKS

David Gray writing about Mary Erskine's in Edinburgh, the oldest school in Britain founded specifically for girls, points out that the 17th Century curriculum at that school included most of what we consider important today, with the addition (surely universally desirable) of thrift, and the cultivation of good sense. His scheme (not unique, I know, but unusual) for the co-education of junior pupils, followed by single-sex classes between the ages of 12 and 16, followed in turn by a co-educational sixth-form, might be worth a wider trial elsewhere.

The essays in this little volume bring into high relief the successes and failures of school education. The schools represented here are clearly better than they were three quarters of a century ago. The education they provide is broader, more humane and more fun. The evidence of their current Heads is that within their schools good things are happening. They do not allow League Tables to squeeze out inspiration and turn them into joyless factories. On the other hand the problems of the past have not disappeared. The education of the least educable is still often a failure. We are still obsessed with measuring results rather than educating people. We face the handicap of antagonism to selection and academic excellence.

The truth about the best schools – those represented here and a few hundred others – is that they are nearly all independent and fee-paying. It is not difficult to see why they succeed. It is a question of size (none is too big). It is a question of teachers who want to teach there and families which want their sons and daughters to be students there. It is a question of vision (which these Heads have in plenty) and a determination to reach the highest standards – academically, in all manner of activities and in the stimulation of young personalities.

Above all it is about having the independence to teach as they believe best and to attract parents who want for their children what the school offers.

All independent schools would like to be more widely available. But when they dispose of only 7% of all the school places in the country, they cannot solve all the inequities of our educational system, however many vouchers and free places are offered. Those merely replace a few lucky pupils whose parents can pay for them with an equal number of lucky pupils whose parents cannot. The real solution is to give greater independence to every school.

It is a tragedy that we do not use our independent schools as exemplars. By any measure they are among the best schools in the world. Their characteristics are not difficult to analyze or imitate. It is only political dogma and an over-centralized educational bureaucracy that prevent our schools from adopting and adapting their strategies for success. It is our loss as a country that they are not encouraged to do so, and a loss to incalculable numbers of young people who deserve the best education we can give them. When a third version of *The Head Speaks* appears in around 2085, how wonderful it would be if it was able to report that all schools by then shared the values and the success of those represented here.

Eric Anderson

[Sir Eric Anderson taught at Fettes and Gordonstoun before becoming successively Head Master of Abingdon, Shrewsbury and Eton. After six years as Rector of Lincoln College, Oxford, he returned to Eton for a further eight years as Provost.]

INTRODUCTION

Julian Lovelock

The Head Master Speaks and The Head Mistress Speaks

The Head Master Speaks was published in 1936 by Kegan Paul, Trench, Trubner & Co. Ltd. My copy has a faded red cloth cover with gold lettering, solid but understated. I discovered it amidst a pile of detritus when more than quarter of a century ago I became a Head Master myself. I tucked it into my bookcase, sensing that it contained wisdom that might indeed be useful. To my shame it was not until my head-mastering days were over that, too late, I found time to learn lessons from such illustrious forebears.

The contributors to that original volume represent a cross-section of 'Public Schools', and their subjects are wide-ranging:

V. P. Nevill, O.S.B. (Ampleforth College): 'A Catholic View'

J. E. Barton (Bristol Grammar School): 'Instruction and Civilization'

N. Whatley (Clifton College): 'Education for 'Citizenship'

A. H. Ashcroft (Fettes College): 'Discipline'

F. Roydon Richards (Glasgow Academy): 'A Plea for Modernity'

Douglas Miller (Manchester Grammar School): 'The School and the Community'

M. L. Jacks (Mill Hill): 'Education for Tomorrow'

J. T. Christie (Repton School): 'The Christian Background'

Hugh Lyon (Rugby School): 'Whither?'

John Bell (St Paul's School): 'Aims and Problems'

J. F. Roxburgh (Stowe School): 'The Public Schools and the Future'

H. N. P. Sloman (Tonbridge School): 'Education Today'

But there is no clue to how the contributors were selected – indeed the editor is entirely invisible. Why, one wonders, are only two of the nine 'Clarendon Schools' (Rugby and St. Paul's) included? Perhaps because the point was to have a 'spread' of schools – geographic, day and boarding, academic and less academic? Or perhaps simply because the Clarendon Head Masters turned down their invitations? And were there suggestions or instructions as to what topics should be addressed? Some themes do run through the volume, but this is more likely to be the result of shared concerns at a particular time than because of editorial edict.

The title *The Head Master Speaks* hints that this is a collection of speeches. It would not be surprising: many Head Masters spend a disproportionate amount of time preparing their 'Speech Day' address, the annual chance to convince parents that they have made the right choice, that their fees are well spent, and that their children's education is in safe hands. But although the contributions are perceptive and often lively, the tightness of their arguments, and indeed their length, would probably have lulled even the most appreciative audience to a post-prandial forty-winks, while the cream teas waited sweltering in the sunshine. No, these are surely more sober considerations of education, at once visionary and practical, concerned more with the education of the nation than with publicity for one school.

A companion volume, *The Head Mistress Speaks*, was published in 1937 (reprinted in 1993 by John Catt Educational Ltd). Here the contributions are both more messianic in tone and more practical. While the Head Masters struggle against complacency, you gain the impression that these formidable Head Mistresses are part of a crusade: education as the foundation of equal rights for women. Yet at the same time the Head Mistresses are more down to earth, more aware of the mechanics of education, of the difficulties of putting theory into practice. Above all they seem more concerned for the individual pupil: you have the sense that as they write they have this particular girl or that particular family firmly in mind.

It is striking, too, how these Head Mistresses almost all espouse the cause of freedom in education: the schools they ran would probably seem rigid and authoritarian to the modern eye, yet they argue for an idyll where girls can (and should) challenge authority, be free to make mistakes and learn from them, take time out from lessons to walk and talk; and where examinations are put firmly in their place. Contributors to *The Head Mistress Speaks* are a more eclectic group than the Head Masters, with Whalley Range Municipal High and Streatham Hill Secondary happily rubbing shoulders with Edinburgh

Ladies' College and St. Paul's Girls':

Christine Arscott (Whalley Range Municipal High School, Manchester): 'Some Principles and a Practice'

M. Dorothy Brock (Mary Datchelor School, Camberwell): 'The Creed of a Headmistress'

M. G. Clarke (Manchester High School): 'Feminine Challenge in Education'

Muriel Davies (Streatham Secondary School): 'The County Secondary School and its Service to the Community'

E. R. Gwatkin (Streatham Hill High School): 'Freedom and Co-operation'

D. F. P. Hiley (Central Newcastle High School): 'The Soil, the Seed and the Sower'

Edith Ironside (Sunderland High School): 'Quo Vadimus?'

H. Lister (Selhurst Grammar School for Girls): 'Towards Freedom'

Cicely E. Robinson (Howell's School, Denbigh): 'An Educational Quest'

L. E. Savill (High School for Girls, Lincoln): 'Differentness'

Ethel Strudwick (St Paul's Girls' School): 'The School and Life'

Mary Tweedie (Edinburgh Ladies' College): 'The Changing Face of Education and its Abiding Spirit'

W. A. Whiting (Bromley County School): 'Societies Well Ordained and Disciplined'

By 1936 and 1937 the Public Schools had come a long way since their Victorian predecessors. It was only a hundred years since, in *Tom Brown's Schooldays*, Tom was being bullied and roasted by Flashman and his acolytes; but influenced by Thomas Arnold, Rugby's great Head Master, the Public Schools had changed, and in 1864 the Clarendon Commission was able to report:

> The course of study has been enlarged; the methods of teaching have been improved; the proportion of masters to boys has been increased; the quantity of work exacted is greater than it was, though still in too many cases less than it ought to be. At the same time the advance in moral and religious training has more than kept pace with that which has been made in intellectual discipline. The old roughness of manners has in a great measure disappeared, and with it the petty tyranny and thoughtless cruelty which were formerly too common, and which used indeed to be thought inseparable from the life of a public school. The boys are better lodged and better cared for, and more attention is paid to their wealth and comfort.

As the rising middle class demanded more and better education for their children, the established Public Schools expanded rapidly and new ones began: nearly fifty schools were founded between 1830 and 1870 alone. The Church – or factions of it – was keen to exert its influence. So, for example, the first of the high church Woodard Schools were founded between 1848 and 1891 by the Reverend Nathaniel Woodard, Curate of Shoreham, specifically for the education of middle class boys (Lancing, Hurstpierpoint and Ardingly all started in the vicarage at Shoreham), while in 1923 the Reverend Warrington, vicar of Monkton Combe, established Canford and Stowe as the first of the Allied Schools, a more evangelical foundation. But with the ending of the First World War attitudes towards the Public Schools changed, and (often not without cause) they came to be seen as self-satisfied, authoritarian places, more interested in 'Games' than academic work, and out of touch with the real world. Indeed it was not until the end of the twentieth century that such practices as beating (by boys as well as masters) and 'fagging' finally came to an end.

However in 1936–1937 state provision of secondary education was still something of a lottery. The secondary curriculum – centred on the Classics – hardly catered for most pupils; and (except in Scotland, where there was a more enlightened approach) the focus for girls remained largely on preparation for the home and domestic service.

Elementary school attendance had been made compulsory in 1880, though it was not free until 1891 and in some districts children could still leave school to go into employment at the age of ten. In due course it became customary for many children to stay on at the elementary schools after the official school leaving age (usually twelve), and some schools developed classes to cater for these. They were known as 'higher grade' schools. So it was that the working classes demanded secondary education for all, a demand supported by the 1895 Bryce Commission. The 1902 Education Act, often considered to be the real beginning of secondary education, empowered councils to finance such education from rates if they thought it desirable, but in fact few councils saw it as a priority. When war broke out in 1914, secondary education for the masses was still no more than a possibility and a dream. It was not until the end of another war that R. A. Butler's 1944 Education Act ushered in at last a coherent national system.

Curriculum, Discipline and Citizenship

Three main themes dominate the thoughts of the Head Masters and Head Mistresses of 1936 – 1937: examinations and the curriculum, discipline (at a time when the media was beginning to exert an undue influence and parents were seemingly abrogating their responsibilities), and what might broadly be called 'Citizenship'. Is it surprising that the same themes should be of equal concern to parents today – though our contributors focus mainly on the first?

Seventy years ago, V. S. Nevill of Ampleforth worried that 'the love of learning may be lost in a sordid struggle to pass examinations', while John Bell of St Paul's School agreed that 'examinations are an inadequate test of a boy's accomplishments, and it is unfortunate that they loom so large in the life of nearly every school'. F. Roydon Richards (Glasgow Academy) worried that important things like 'citizenship, religion, aesthetic culture and contact with reality' were being squeezed out by the pressure of examinations, which were no longer the 'nurslings of universities' but had been 'spoiled by the undiscriminating embrace of the layman'. N. Whatley (Clifton College) condemned 'the attempt to get through a particular examination boys who are not suited for it', but he warned against a move to a 'one-size-fits-all' solution: 'It will be a thousand pities if examinations become easier and easier in the interest of less able boys and too little is demanded of able boys'. Did he foresee today's apparent lowering of standards at A level and GCSE? The Head Mistresses agreed. Christing Arscott (Whalley Range Municipal High School) claimed that 'examination conditions have almost strangled experiment outside the framework of the traditional curriculum'. Cicely Robinson (Howell's School) attacked 'the strait-jacket of examinations: 'Even the very best schools cannot provide ideal teaching .... so long as outside bodies .... compel girls to grind at subjects that defy retention in the mind once the examination is over'. And Mary Tweedie (Edinburgh Ladies' College) was angry that education had become 'the attainment at all costs of some ill-defined quantity of examinable knowledge to be pressed into the school and University years'.

A. H. Ashcroft (Fettes College) worried about a curriculum that was becoming broader but more superficial, so boys were being 'taught to read but not to think': '.... far too many boys are allowed to get some way in many subjects rather than a long way in three or four'. This was a view shared by Douglas Miller (Manchester Grammar School) who acknowledged that 'a narrow pedantic course of study .... is wrong' but that you do not 'gain breadth by merely increasing the number of subjects studied', and by H. N. P. Sloman (Tonbridge School) who believed that schools 'teach too much, with the inevitable result that some boys have no time to learn'. In the same vein, Miss Hiley (Central Newcastle High School) noted that 'We have …. fixed our attention on the field of knowledge, not on the child …. A healthy diet does not attempt to include everything good to eat'; and Muriel Davies (Streatham Secondary School) worried about 'an overdose of education'. Surprisingly (for a modern reader) J. E. Barton (Bristol Grammar School) wanted more state control of education, hoping that the power of universities, examination boards and other vested interests would be diminished, thus liberating schools from 'the academic tyranny, and from the chaos of specialized learning and syllabus-mongering which now goes on practically unchecked, with an almost sublime indifference to the total needs of the actual boy as a person'. The majority of contributors urged the inclusion of Music, Art and Drama in the curriculum.

Writing before Butler's 1944 Education Act, two contributors pondered the future shape of secondary education. Christine Arscott supported a system of Grammar and Modern Schools; though admitting that 'a single multi-bias school for all …. from certain points of view would be more ideal', she concluded that such a school would be too large and amorphous. On the other hand, Muriel Davies condemned selection at 11+ until an 'equally good alternative training is provided for those who do not win places in secondary schools'.

Although V. P. Nevill believed that discipline (along with religion and sound learning) was one of the three things that Public Schools stood for, he warned that too many rules and regulations 'beget a habit of evasion if not a sense of grievance'. Miss Gwatkin (Streatham Hill High School), in a remarkably enlightened article for the time, went much further, believing that 'a reasonable standard of politeness in the school should make extremes of bad behaviour impossible', and urging that it is freedom that should be encouraged:

> Freedom means freedom to do wrong as well as freedom to do
> right: girls can only learn to use their powers by using them,
> and inevitably they will misuse them at times. Such misuse
> may be a great nuisance and that is how it should be treated,
> not as a sign of moral turpitude.

Cicely Robinson agreed: 'As freedom is essential to all true development, rigid external discipline must disappear from school life'. However Douglas Miller noted that although boys had more independence than their predecessors, they were 'less inclined to stand up to the hard issues of life'; and A. H. Ashcroft held that 'simplicity is an essential in disciplined life' and deplored 'the tendency to make the comforts of school approximate very closely to those of home'.

Today we worry about children spending their time in front of computers and television, and about the undue influence of the media. In 1936 – 1937, 'wireless' rather than television was the problem, but the effect was the same. John Bell spoke of the need to teach young people to think for themselves 'in these days of slogans and advertisements', while H. N. P. Sloman warned that 'the vast power of mass suggestion wielded by those who control the Wireless and the Press, whether private individuals or governments, is one of the most sinister features of the modern world'.

M. L. Jacks thought the same: in an age where manipulation by the media was a huge danger, he stressed the importance of teaching boys to think – something often achieved more easily in traditional school subjects rather than in more 'supposedly useful subjects' which threatened to oust them from the curriculum. Edith Ironside (Sunderland High School) complained of the 'cult of amusement' and of how 'Conversation, Music, Reading .... are banished by mechanized amusement'. Ethel Strudwick (St Paul's Girls School) was concerned about the intrusion of 'wireless' on family life and on homework.

But on the matter of discipline perhaps the most common thread running through all the contributions was the need for the active support and involvement of parents. V. P. Nevill believed that 'nothing can be achieved without the support of parents'. J. T. Christie (Repton) noted that 'there is far more friendliness between sons and fathers than there was, but there is also less respect on the one hand and less deliberate training and guidance on the other' – leaving the school 'to stand *in loco parentis* to a degree that Thomas Arnold never dreamed of'. Miss Clarke agreed, saying that 'more is demanded of the school than it is in a position to give' and stressing the need for the home to be 'fully rehabilitated as an educational factor'. Edith Ironside worried that parents were withholding 'the guidance that they are obviously in a position to give' and Mary Tweedie emphasized that 'confidence between home and school is an essential ingredient of good work'.

Writing in a society altered almost beyond recognition by the First World War, and in the shadow of another impending conflict, contributors to the original volumes debate the area of 'Citizenship' – though for them the term has a far wider connotation than it does today. M. L. Jacks wrote of the rapid changes in society and the need not to educate boys for the present (as opposed to the past), but rather 'for the world as it *will* be'. He looked towards a more international community in which 'power, patriotism and citizenship will have to be reinterpreted' and argued the need for widening the social catchment of the Public Schools. N. Whatley believed that 'citizenship' should not be yet another specialist subject on the curriculum, but that every subject should include instruction in citizenship (would that today's educational legislators had listened to him!); but in an essay entitled 'Education for Citizenship' he worried that 'Schools are increasingly pleasant places for the weak: I doubt that they demand enough of the strong'.

Muriel Davies suggested that 'education should be a slower process, and a far more all-round one, including a fuller study and practice of human relationships'. In the same vein, Ethel Strudwick argued that 'in a world that has rarely been in a greater mess' it was important to show that 'self-restraint and a mutual tolerance make for happiness on the small stage of the school world, and so prepare them for the larger stage on which those qualities will have ample scope'. Cicely Robinson agreed that 'relationships, personal, national and international' matter more than anything else in life. In a maturing democracy John Bell understood the need to arouse in the voter of tomorrow 'a real, practical interest in public affairs', while on a practical level H. N. P. Sloman proposed that 'Essay Writing and Newspaper periods, with précis work at a slightly later stage, should be .... the basis of all our education. A. H. Ashcroft lamented that 'Public School Old Boys do not play the part in national life that might reasonably be expected of them'.

As one might expect, the majority of contributors place Christianity at the heart of education. For example, Miss Hiley asked: 'Is it not the prime duty of the school to keep alive …. spiritual awareness and give it an atmosphere in which it can flourish without ridicule on the one hand or mawkish interest on the other?' J. H. Christie saw the threat posed to Christianity by both Communism and National Socialism – and how without 'the superhuman spirit of Christianity' all education would become political education. But some saw uncomfortable ironies. He wondered 'whether the *Public School spirit* is really compatible with true Christianity' and Hugh Lyon attacked the notion of building character – something that excuses 'so many cruelties and barbarisms'. What matters, argued Lyon, is 'the education of the spirit', which is 'much more than what is commonly called religious education'.

But it is in Miss Clarke that – through her writings – I find a soul-mate from across the years. Miss Clarke is clear that a Head is no more or less than a first among equals. It is the Head's job to liberate and empower his or her teachers, the 'most precious asset' of any school, so that they are not weighed down by the 'false standards' of examination results, nor by 'excessive reverence for the letter of regulations or nervousness of officialdom'. 'The very real enemy of the teacher's freedom is overconscientiousness in the Head!' writes Miss Clarke. She goes on:

Organization should leave as many loopholes as possible for the initiative of the staff to fill, whether in the planning of schemes and syllabuses or in the day-to-day arrangements of the school. There are, in fact, two great guides to conduct for all school administrators, which may startle those brought up on the maxims of the Victorian copybook: 'Do nothing yourself that you can get someone else to do for you', and: 'Do nothing today that you can put off till tomorrow!' But, in caring for these, the Head is caring effectively for the freedom of the staff.

The Head Speaks: Challenges and Visions in Education

To compile the current volume I approached the Head Masters or Head Mistresses of all those schools represented in 1936 and 1937 which still exist in a recognizable form. I asked them for their view on the challenges facing their schools and their vision for the future. Specifically I asked for contributions which are general rather than particular to individual schools (though inevitably, being Heads, some have skirted round even this request!). There was no expectation that the contributors would tackle the same themes as their predecessors: I was looking for their thoughts, now, and not for dry comparisons.

Although I am immensely grateful to our contributors, many of whose essays make an important contribution to educational debate, I have to own up to some disappointments about the present volume – not, of course, because of what it includes, but because of what it has had to leave out.

First, the fact that only about half of the Heads of the schools represented in 1936 and 1937 have been able to send contributions has meant that the scope of this volume is narrower than that of its predecessors. Did the original anonymous editor have the same difficulty (but a much larger number of potential contributors)? Or is it a reflection of the changed role of the Head Teacher in the twenty-first century, where management has become as important as leadership, and where time that seventy years ago might have been spent reflecting on education (or indeed in the class-room) is now taken up by the demands of compliance with central government policy, health and safety, employment law, committees and a mound of paperwork besides? The comparatively recent introduction of national training for Head Teachers recognizes and consolidates the changed role of the Head (as does the return of the suggestion that Heads could usefully be drawn from outside the teaching profession). It might be more appropriate for many of a Head Teacher's management tasks to be delegated to suitably qualified subordinates, freeing him or her to concentrate again on genuinely educational challenges – and on inspiring staff, pupils and communities. As John Bell, the High Master of St Paul's, put it in 1936: '.... where there is no vision, the people perish'.

The volume is also diminished because the Heads of only two girls' schools – The Mary Erskine School (formerly the Edinburgh Ladies' College) and Sunderland High School – have written for us. A number of the original girls' schools have been amalgamated more than once into other schools or have disappeared altogether, so the field was decimated before we started. Is this a sign that the days of all-girls schools (even of single sex schools) are numbered? It would have been helpful to have had more reports from the front line.

In particular, the volume is diminished because no Head of a maintained school has been able to accept our invitation, so there is no debate about the changes and challenges in state schooling. Do the new Academies represent a sensible way ahead, and how much independence do they really have? Is the grammar school debate over, and are the remaining grammar schools living on borrowed time; or will there be a resurgence as a revolt against mediocrity? Most importantly, how can schools educate children of the new social underclass, who at the moment seem condemned at birth to a sordid culture of guns, knives and drug related crime? It was never the intention that this volume would represent only the independent sector, but that is how it has turned out. I have no doubt that there is room for a further more important book to represent the views of Head Teachers in the maintained system.

However the real disappointment is more fundamental. Although some of our contributors write with justifiable (if usually muted) pride of all the good things that are being achieved in their schools, it is clear that, though some battles have been won, few of the problems of seventy years ago have gone away. In many cases they have become more severe.

The complaints about the negative impact of too many examinations have certainly not been heeded, and the early criticism of the undue influence of the School Certificate pales against our own era, when 'key stage' assessments begin in the primary school, and secondary school pupils are examined almost continuously from the age of fourteen.

The 1936-7 contributors worried that while the curriculum was, by and large, suited to the brightest pupils, those of average and below average ability were ill catered for. It is undoubtedly true that the secondary curriculum remains unsuited to too many pupils, and this will remain the case as long as vocational qualifications carry with them both academic and social stigma. (In the same way, the secondary modern school was never allowed to develop as it should have done, and the introduction of the comprehensive school was in large part the result of pressure from middle class parents whose children were not selected for grammar school education.) The new 'Diploma', which might have been an answer to the conundrum, seems to offer the worst of all worlds and it might be kinder for everyone if it died in its infancy.

But able children have been let down as well, and N. Whatley's worry that doing the right thing for less able children might result in a dumbing down for all has come horribly true. In the current book, the High Masters of both Manchester Grammar School and St Paul's School, Dr Christopher Ray and Dr Martin Stephen, argue fiercely for the upholding of academic standards.

In spite of a number of local initiatives, a steady increase in the amount of financial help offered to less well-off families by schools, and the new demands of the Charities' Commission, the gulf between the maintained and state sector seems wider than ever. The Direct Grant Scheme and the Assisted Places Scheme offered routes for children from poorer homes into independent schools, but both were discontinued by Labour governments who viewed them as an unnecessary financial drain on the maintained sector. Here, Dr

Dominic Luckett, Head Master of Mill Hill, returns to ponder this problem which was raised by his 1936 predecessor, and Dr Anthony Wallersteiner, Head Master of Stowe, posits educational vouchers as a possible solution.

Patrick Derham, Head Master of Rugby School, rightly (in my view) identifies the current tendency of Public Schools to compete with each other in providing the best of facilities – sports halls, swimming pools, and the like – as a major cause of the independent sector becoming, if anything, more exclusive. Public Schools are, of course, driven by the market, but it would be a disaster if they were to become even more the preserve of the few. It remains to be seen whether the new commercially backed groups of schools (for the most part buying out individual proprietors, and benefiting from economies of scale), which are beginning to occupy the less expensive end of the independent school market, will be successful enough to influence the approach of the established Public Schools. Good schools should be good businesses, but good businesses will not necessarily run good schools.

The battle to establish Music, Art and Drama as part of the secondary curriculum has largely been won, and here Peter Brodie, the Rector of The Glasgow Academy, writes passionately of the importance of such subjects. Mr Brodie also argues the importance of architecture and space, and along with almost every other contributor recognizes that outstanding teachers are the life-blood of any school. One of the major challenges of the past twenty-five years has been the growth of Information Technology and the need to incorporate it at the centre of the curriculum. This is charted in detail by Dr David

Mascord of Bristol Grammar School and considered at some length by Dr. Angela Slater of Sunderland High School. In recounting the history of The Mary Erskine School, David Gray shows how schools have evolved to meet ever changing needs, and suggests one solution to the single-sex versus co-education debate. Fr Gabriel Everitt tells of the importance of religion – and faith – in schools, and of the Benedictine tradition in his own school, Ampleforth College.

With such a diversity of subjects – and with some contributors ranging widely – any attempt to group contributions according to subject would fail, so I have followed the example of the original volumes and set out contributions in alphabetical order of author. I am immensely grateful to Sir Eric Anderson for his wise and inspiring Foreword, to Christopher Woodhead of the University of Buckingham Press for shouldering much of the administrative burden, and to my Buckingham colleagues Dr Terence Kealey and Professor John Clarke for their advice.

I have no doubt that today, as in 1936–1937, the independent sector has a huge part to play in influencing the direction of education in the United Kingdom. Because it is independent, it can to an extent think about education free from government intervention and restraint. Independent schools can choose their own curriculum, can decide which examinations pupils sit, can set standards of behaviour and discipline which parents and pupils are bound (and choose) to accept and champion. Schools like St. Paul's and Manchester Grammar can set the bar for academic standards; other schools (like Summerhill – I wish our format had allowed one of the 'progressive' schools to be represented) can point the way to a genuinely alternative way of doing things. Everyone can learn from both extremes. Above all, independent schools can offer real choice – though only to those who can afford their fees. It is more vital than ever that they use their independence constructively and do not become pale but expensive and exclusive copies of the best maintained schools.

But although independent schools have an important role to play in the nation's education, it is foolish and patronizing to pretend that they have much to teach a comprehensive school in a deprived inner city area; bursaries, or vouchers, or whatever, might offer a ladder from one world to another for a selected few – and that might be worthwhile – but they will not begin to alter the educational landscape. While it would be presumptuous of me even to enter into the debate about the future direction of maintained schools, it is the philosophy of this book that it is Head Masters and Head Mistresses of vision, who know their pupils as individuals, rather than a distant central government, who are best equipped to point the way.

So I end by reiterating that we need above all leaders and not managers for our schools, independent and maintained. We must listen to them and not to the army of theorists and bureaucrats who would emasculate them. In 1936, N. Whatley of Clifton College wrote:

> Best of all perhaps would be the appearance on the scene of a really great Head Master   a man of vision, strength and courage, a public figure but not a showman, a man who can see both wood and trees, at once prophet, scholar and statesman. There are many good Head Masters in England – the average has perhaps never been so high – but it would not

be unfair to say that they are administrators rather than prophets. It is long since there was an outstandingly great Head Master. Is this to be the permanent fate of all professions in Modern England?

His call is even more urgent today.

University of Buckingham   ***July, 2008***

[Julian Lovelock was for quarter of a century Head Master of Akeley Wood School, Buckingham (an independent co-educational day school of some 900 pupils aged 3 –18). He is now Chief Operating Officer at the University of Buckingham, where he also lectures in English Literature. Among his many publications is *Education and Democracy* (Routledge, 1975), which he edited jointly with A.E. Dyson.]

AMPLEFORTH COLLEGE

'A CATHOLIC VIEW' (1936)

V. P. Nevill, OSB

Although in 1937 the Reverend V. P. Nevill wrote specifically from a Roman Catholic standpoint, he took it that all Public Schools 'stand for three things: religion, discipline and sound learning'.

'Religious teaching,' Father Nevill argued, 'must be clear, frank and dogmatic; it is no good trying to disguise it by giving a boy religion as our Victorian mothers gave us medicine, hidden under a mouthful of plum jam.' He also stressed the importance of a common standard between home and school.

On discipline, Father Nevill suggested perceptively that, 'A boy must have liberty if he is to practise virtue, but liberty must be graduated and consistent with his age and knowledge'. He condemned 'general laws for the moral guidance of boys': a wise master will know each boy and treat him as an individual. In the same way he insisted that 'it is a mistake to give boys too many rules and regulations to live by .... there is always a danger of over-legalizing and thereby merely tantalizing by pettifogging regulations'. But (lest Father Nevill is portrayed as a rather wet liberal), there is a warning note too: 'Public spirit is fostered by the presence of tradition and the

1

application of reasonable sanctions consecrated by wise traditional methods'.

Today's teachers will sympathize with Father Nevill's assertion that, 'The love of learning and scholarship may be lost in a sordid struggle to pass examinations' and with his lament that study of the English language has been forced out by an unbalanced curriculum: 'The inability of so many boys to express themselves clearly and logically in their own tongue is one of the penalties of our having to overload the IV Form [year 10] timetable'.

Finally Father Nevill pointed to recent improvements in Public Schools – the improvement of living conditions so that boys have 'decent and dignified surroundings'; the opportunities to acquire an interest in Music, Art and Drama; the fostering of creative and manual skills; the greater importance of 'Games' in providing a channel into which to direct physical energy (though there is a warning against the worship of 'mere athletic prowess'). Even in 1937, however, there were siren calls offering unwanted distractions:

'Jazz', the cinema, and motor-car, speedboat and aeroplane periodicals tend to absorb too much of a boy's attention and provide something of a problem, which every school must solve in its own way. They cannot be wholly taboo, or they acquire the interest and attraction of forbidden fruit.

In the twenty-first century the distractions may be different, but the problem is the same, and there remains no easy solution.

A CATHOLIC AND BENEDICTINE VIEW

Fr Gabriel Everitt OSB

There is much debate about what constitutes a good school. Today attention is often focused on league tables, though many realize that a higher league table position does not always guarantee a better school; it may simply mean, for example, a school with a more selective entry. Schools acquire, and can lose, reputations as 'good' and certainly recommendation by parents of current pupils is a key for the promotion of schools. Parents, who love their children, want them to be happy and successful, two considerations easy to say but difficult to pin down.

For all of us in education, our task and our responsibility remains the same: to help prepare the child for his or her adult life, to provide the structures, guidance and support for the shaping of each child's intellectual, physical and spiritual development. This is what a good school does, and its measure of success is the quality of the young people it has prepared for the world. A bad school will have failed in these objectives, or worse, will have never addressed them, maybe accepting in sullen apathy its lot as a sink school devoid of hope or aspiration; or, at the other end of the academic scale, focusing its objectives so keenly on the single target of exam performance that the moral, social, spiritual and true intellectual life of its pupils warp and atrophy through neglect.

Schools are much inspected today and therefore they are very accountable; they need to have a clear view, and communicate well with their various 'stakeholders'. Schools need to promote very actively their current strengths and to have a clear view on how they are going to improve still further. The dominant impression in schools, as in the educational world generally, can be one of restlessness. This is not necessarily a bad thing; though the world of education can be a tiring and a frustrating one today for all concerned.

Indeed the pace of change seems to accelerate, so that when one looks back seventy years to the era of *The Head Master Speaks*, it can appear to be a far distant one. Father Paul Nevill, the Head Master of Ampleforth at that time, contributed a 'Catholic' view, in which he saw the heart of the public school system in religion, discipline and sound learning.

The latter two are probably still be on most lists today, reassuring us that while much changes, much remains the same: fundamental values abide. I want to spend a good part of this article thinking about religion, but I cannot resist first noting how much it is a case of 'plus ça change, plus c'est la même chose' in the matter of 'sound learning'. Fr Paul noted the value of examinations, in his case the School Certificate, though his attitude was rather that public examinations were a necessary evil. He wrote, 'A school is judged good or bad by the number of its examination successes; parental pressure is brought to bear upon schools to cram knowledge into boys or to rush early examinations at a time when they would be better occupied in learning to think'.

How true still. Yes, of course, academic excellence is always one of the attributes you will look for in a school, but it is a mistake to confuse a talent for exam grade delivery with true academic excellence. More and more it does seem that our education system is being shoe-horned into the confines of grade delivery, rather than educational excellence. So, there is a temptation for schools to focus on techniques of grade enhancement, rather than nurturing love and understanding of the subject. Of course these need not be mutually exclusive, but they are now too easily divorced.

We have never had a generation of children so tested as this school generation of today. But I remain unconvinced that this has contributed any serious improvement to the quality of education offered in our schools. In fact, I think a strong case could be made that in important areas of education, the exam, test and grade approach has impoverished education, and may be actually damaging the future success of the child.

The pressure of league tables and the hunger for grades are remorselessly turning A Levels into ends in themselves. They should never be that. For the young man or woman going on to university, A level studies should have provided the opportunity to learn disciplines of study and perhaps love of the subject which will carry them through the foothills of their university career, and beyond. But the temptation now is to focus on exam technique and grade enhancement, rather than on knowledge and understanding. For the parent concerned about their child's success, this could be the worm in the rose. Yes, the A level results may be all they wished, and university entrance may follow, but if the child has been grade-groomed, rather than truly educated, the price will be paid at university.

In fact, as I have said, there is no reason why exam performance and true education need follow different routes. One of the most exciting things in education can be to see the result of a fine teacher inspiring love of the subject in his or her pupils. If you have a passion to educate, the exam grades will take care of themselves. But I fear that a culture geared to tests and measurement, rather than to true education, is taking root now, and it has the potential to inflict great damage.

But what of religion, the first of Fr Paul's hallmarks of a school? Here there seems to have been a significant change. It is of course true that Fr Paul thought of himself as being somewhat 'out on a limb' and maybe more so than Catholics might feel today. He recognized that as a Catholic priest and a Benedictine he would not be 'considered a typical exponent of the Public School system'. He would not, however, have considered himself, I think, as belonging to a sub-group within the educational system of 'faith schools'. Indeed in discussing religion as a foundation of schooling at the beginning of his article, he was seeking common ground with his 'brother head masters', not looking for something that would set him apart. Today it is different; faith schools are perceived to be apart from the 'rest', they promote particular beliefs, not necessarily common values. They are applauded in some cases for good results and high standards of discipline, but criticised in others for creedal and social division.

In a changed world religion is less emphasized, suggesting as it does that which divides. An attempt has been made to replace religion with 'spirituality', something which it is thought can apply to all schools, not just to 'faith schools'. Thus school inspectors are required to look into the spiritual development of pupils. Inspectors have required some training in what to look for and schools are needing to consider what it is that inspectors will be hoping to find. Recent guidance from the Independent Schools Inspectorate suggests that:

> Spiritual development is the development of the non-material element of being human which sustains individuals and, depending on their point of view, either ends or continues in some form when they die. It is about the development of a sense of identity, self-worth, personal insight, meaning and purpose. It is about the development of a 'spirit'. Some people may call it the development of a pupil's 'soul'; others, the development of 'personality' or 'character'.

It is good that an attempt is made to locate the 'spiritual'. In an age of relativism and social confusion, it can be horribly difficult to peer through the moral murk. Young people leaving school today must at times feel that the society they have entered has lost any moral compass. They will find a society where celebrity has become more valued than achievement; where leadership is no longer driven by belief and principle, but by expediency and focus groups. They will find a society where the concepts of duty, honour, even honesty, have been undermined by the new cynicism, increasingly replaced by 'rights' and nourished by sour resentment. Those schools which have held to their beliefs and their principles, and which continue to provide a strong spiritual and moral core to their education, may be providing their children with exactly the resources they need to navigate their way through adult life in this increasingly confusing and uncertain world.

For Catholic schools, Jesus Christ is at the centre. For some other schools too of course, but this has been a strong emphasis in Roman Catholic writing about education over the past forty years. The Congregation for Catholic Education document, *The Religious Dimension of Education in a Catholic School* (1988), puts it in the following way: 'In a Catholic school, everyone should be aware of the living presence of Jesus the 'Master' who, today as always, is with us in our journey through life as the one genuine 'Teacher', the perfect Man in whom all human values find their fullest perfection. The inspiration of Jesus must be translated from the ideal into the real.' The Catholic emphasis is not to get the faithful few into the fortress and pull up the drawbridge. The Catholic ideal, having put Christ at the centre, is to go out in service to others and part of this service is to respond to an age of spiritual need.

Are there insights from a Benedictine tradition which can particularly help to give shape to the concept of a pupil's spiritual development? Hardly surprisingly I think there are. St Benedict wrote a guide for monastic communities which he described as a 'small rule for beginners'. He was probably not thinking too far beyond his own country of Italy or his own time of the sixth century, but his rule has provided a sure guide line for community living down to our own time and recently many, not just monks and nuns or Catholics, have looked to it for guidance for living. Hence a growth in the number of books which apply Benedictine ideals to the life of lay men and women. I have myself found these attempts very interesting and helpful, not least in the task of applying Benedictine ideals to a school, which after all is a community made up of lay pupils and increasingly today lay teachers.

It may be worth mentioning at the outset that St Benedict was very realistic in legislating for his community of monks, indeed this is one of the features which has guaranteed his Rule such a long life. His monks could be a wayward lot just like any group of human souls and just like pupils in any school. It is clear for example that St Benedict's monks sometimes drank too much, they found it hard to get out of bed in the morning and their eagerness for work sometimes needed a little encouragement. Hence the importance of a rule. It was a rule that St Benedict attempted to impose fairly, sometimes strictly, albeit with an eye to individual need and character.

Benedictine elements in education are less a programme and more an atmosphere and an environment. This may make them hard to isolate and describe but perhaps a few key aspects may be mentioned. A first is a special commitment to community: the highest value should be placed on relationships and life together. A school is a community made up of different personalities. Each student, each parent, each member of staff, each monk comes with his or her own story, vulnerabilities and hopes. The aim should be to welcome and to include them all, to offer an environment where respect for one another comes to life. The importance of community can be widely shared among educators today, as it is readily understood by many that education is not just imparting knowledge to an individual, which could perhaps be done most conveniently and economically behind a computer screen at home. But individuals are prepared for a life in society and with others by being educated 'together', with all that entails. It takes a community to educate a child. This is perhaps one of the truest measures and most important contributions of any good school. Where in our adult society the sense of community is so often reduced to a narrow, angry tribalism, a true sense of community celebrates the value of service, generosity, sacrifice, responsibility, patience, understanding and love. If as educators we achieve nothing else, but succeed in putting the building blocks in place for a true and healthy community, then we will not have failed.

Another Benedictine emphasis is balance; a word which is often used when describing the Rule. Benedict creates the opportunity for a balanced day. Work, prayer, private study and time with others all find their place. It is a great gift if in our hectic lives with so many demands and so much noise, there can be some commitment to prayer as an easy and natural part of daily life. Prayer can underpin the busy school life and brings a sense of order to it. It can give an awareness of others, near and far, known or unknown, important in a culture that says each for themselves. I think it is a great pity when worship becomes just yet more words. I think that young people and their teachers can benefit from some short time of guided silence in their lives. For a Catholic school, the celebration of Mass will be the source and summit of the school's life of prayer; a Mass in which pupils are given a very active part can be a most powerful and moving witness to the life of faith.

As well as prayer, there certainly is a need for good and frequent communication, the art of having a talk, the appeal to the fact that each individual is created and loved, and a patient attention to the art of community living. While the absence of respect and its perversions can, we may hope, be restrained by sanction, Benedict was speaking of something that goes beyond law and rule and which cannot be imposed – much as St Paul was when he wrote to the Galatians of 'love, joy, peace, patience, kindness, goodness, trustfulness, gentleness and self control' and then went on to say, 'No law can touch such things as these'. One might say no amount of micro-management by bossy government or indeed bossy headmaster is guaranteed, or indeed likely, to capture and change hearts, to shape character. But much can be achieved by conversation and patient working together. The good will of the young is still there to be mobilised and sometimes a difficult situation can be changed from within a peer group when this good will is challenged and released. There are elusive balances: the balance of incentive and sanction, of freedom (without which there may seem to be little worthwhile human growth) and protection, of community and individual. Fr Paul Nevill seventy years ago particularly emphasized the role of pupils in the running of a school: 'The English boy shows a remarkable gift for quiet and effective leadership, and I rejoice to see him exercising it. General guidance and advice is always necessary, but I am quite certain that the responsibility and authority entrusted to boys must be real and based on the genuine trust of their head master and housemasters'. Today prefects and captains as well as other pupil office holders can still occupy the same role and gain the same experience. Many schools have discovered the value of a Student

Council. It is intriguing and heartening how constructively a Council can play its part in thinking through important aspects of school development. This too was an insight of St Benedict: 'As often as anything important is to be done in the monastery, the abbot shall call the whole community together and himself explain what the business is; and after hearing the advice of the brothers, let him ponder it and follow what he judges the wiser course. The reason why we have said all should be called for counsel is that the Lord often reveals what is better to the younger'. (Rule of St Benedict chapter 3, 'Summoning the Brothers for Counsel').

'Respect' is a quality once given but more often, these days, angrily demanded. Benedict calls us to show respect to the other and his main 'weapon' in this battle of the heart is humility. It is strange, maybe even it sounds annoyingly sanctimonious or hypocritical, to mention humility in the context of education. In education, where achievement is rightly lauded, and recognition often a spur to success, humility may seem a difficult value to nurture. Where is its place in the annual prize day? Is it a quality you seek in a second row forward? Perhaps not. Finding ourselves doing well in the humility stakes so easily leads us to be proud. Humility is at its best when we look away from ourselves, but in education we cannot look wholly away from ourselves. The educational endeavour wants us to take a good, well-informed, hard long look at how we are progressing as learners. The young do need to look at themselves and to develop a quiet sense of confidence in what they see. They need too to develop the ability to look to others in respect and to look to God as the ground of being.

I think a great key to humility is gratitude, gratitude to others, gratitude to God. St Benedict again says (in his *Tools for Good Works*) 'If you notice something good in yourself, give credit to God, not to yourself'. The adventure is to cure the astigmatism which puts ourselves at the centre and to see ourselves as part of a succession of communities grounded in the creative love of God, of which a school is but one part.

If parents are looking for success for their children, perhaps one of our greatest challenges is also to address the issue of perceived failure. The reality is that in the world for which we are preparing them, these young people will find that success and failure are part of the currency of life. Almost every child will face setbacks and disappointments, difficulties and trials in the course of his or her school career. How they respond to those setbacks, what they learn from them, and how they grow from what they learn should be a central element to any education. As educators, one of our greatest challenges must be to provide our pupils with the resources and inspiration they need to meet adversity and to respond to disappointment with honesty, courage, determination and generosity. Here again the spiritual dimension has a hugely important role to play. Children must learn to find and develop qualities within themselves, but the strength they find in their Faith, and in the love of Christ, can make all the difference when the challenge seems most bleak.

I was much cut down to size – I am sure it was very good for me – when some months ago a new student, seeing me tour the games fields, bade me a cheery welcome and commented to me that, unlike his prep school Head Master, he never seemed to see me. 'What exactly do you do?' he asked. He would not have needed to ask his teachers that and I want to end with a comment on staff.

Teachers need to have some sense of satisfaction in what they do and preferably to enjoy it, if they are really to teach well. It needs to be a work of love. Teachers often grow a carapace of cynicism, they can be gruff and tough. Pupils on the whole have a good sense, however, of when their teachers are genuinely motivated by a desire to see them flourish beneath any surface crustiness. St John Bosco, the founder of the Salesian order, reminds us of this: 'If we want to be thought of as men who have the real happiness of our pupils at heart and who help each to fulfil his role in life, you must never forget that you are taking the place of parents who love their children. I have always worked, studied and exercised my priesthood out of love for them.' To teachers too one can apply advice of St Benedict to the abbot, as it applies to any person entrusted with the care of any community, be that school or family. 'He must hate faults', says St Benedict, 'but love the brothers. When he must punish them, he should use prudence and avoid extremes; otherwise, by rubbing too hard to remove the rust, he may break the vessel … Let him strive to be loved rather than feared.'

BRISTOL GRAMMAR SCHOOL

'INSTRUCTION AND CIVILISATION' (1936)

J. E. Barton

In 1936, J. E. Barton, while acknowledging that there is some truth in the perception of Headmasters as 'a breezily dogmatic type, too busy for self-questioning', nevertheless protests that they are almost inevitably thwarted by external 'obstacles and resistant forces'.

First, he complains of the way education is 'determined by what I hope is not unkind to call middle-class aspirations':

Schoolchildren are sectionalized by the material means and ambitions of their families, and the concept of education as a social and financial lever, rather than as an equipment for the whole art of living, is deep-seated in almost all grades of English society.

So it is that:

The lives of approved teachers and scholars are subtly permeated by the false or at any rate dubious values which have been created by a century of materialism and striving after externals.

Secondly, and in more detail, Barton attacks the control of the curriculum by the universities, which compel schools 'to instruct the general run of boys by standards and methods which belong to academic specialism'. Far from resenting state control, he sees the Board of Education as encouraging initiatives and favouring 'any trend towards a less rigid and more enlightened standard of education as a whole'. Indeed he concludes:

> *Given the right people, I should like to see not less but more of autocratic power: power to create real freedom by liberating us from the academic tyranny, and from the chaos of specialized learning and syllabus-mongering which now goes on practically unchecked, with an almost sublime indifference to the total needs of the actual boy, as a person.*

Barton is especially and fiercely critical of public examinations, which 'are now a large industry and a powerful vested interest'. While people talk of 'freedom and the development of personality', the truth is that 'the growing boy is really at the mercy of teachers who themselves are at the mercy of examiners', ending in disaster for all:

> *Clever boys find they can get marks by parroting abstractions which teachers or text-books offer them ready-made. Ordinary pupils lapse into contentment with a good deal that is only half understood. The boy of sub-average scholastic aptitude is*

often crushed by the burden, though he may be a boy of useful all-round capacity and intelligence of the type which educates itself from experience and observation of life, rather than from books and ordered thinking.

Moreover, Barton argues, 'examinations crowd out all sorts of important interests – physical, social and aesthetic – which we cannot afford to neglect'. Writing before the imposition of SATs, he praises the remarkable achievements of junior schools, which are 'less cramped by academic obsessions'.

Thirdly, with access to secondary schools opened to children from every background, Barton highlights the difficulties for teachers in contending with the attitude with which pupils arrive at school – attitudes born of the new industrial society:

Most children come to school with lovable natures and decent instincts: but their minds have already admitted the baneful effects of inaccurate speech, sensational imagery, cheap facetiousness, sentimental art, soppy literature and herd thinking. To a large extent these vices originate from depravities that were unavoidable in a haphazard industrialism such as that which cursed our country before all others.

So the challenge for schools in 1936, as Barton sees it, is to contribute something towards a new social unity, though he notes the new vertical class distinction between the intelligent minority and 'the *multitude which knows just enough to be commercially exploited and intellectually robotized':*

> *A good schooling would provide spiritual ballast, as well as mental nurture, for the intelligent few. For the mass it should encourage useful habits and sound principles of life, with some sort of distant respect for things of the mind. If such aims were achieved, all alike might share the happiness of a less distracted and positively nobler society.*

THE INFORMATION REVOLUTION
IN SCHOOLS

David Mascord

This is an account of a teacher's journey and his responses to the information revolution. In recording my experiences it is hoped others can avoid my and others' mistakes. When I entered teaching I believed that computers could have a role to play in education, but I could not say that I foresaw either the speed or complexity of the information revolution. I trained as teacher of Chemistry in 1975-6 and took up my first post in September 1976. My background as a Ph.D. student had given me substantial experience of programming computers as well as significant experience of them as a scientific tool. I moved on to a Head of Department post at an independent school, then to a senior teacher post at a maintained grammar school; finally I became first Assistant Head, then Deputy Head, then Head of Bristol Grammar School, an independent, coeducational, selective day school.

The period of my own experience in education has proved to be a time of unprecedented change in both the independent and maintained sectors. The educational world of 1976 was very different from that of 2008. The structure defined by the 1944 Education Act, at least in so far as grammar and secondary schools were concerned, was still discernible. A growing number of comprehensive schools was, however, starting to eat into that division. My own education in the 1960s had been at one of the new comprehensive schools. The third type of school defined by the 1944 Act, the technical school, had never been part of my experience and I only read about these when I trained in 1976.

In 1976 an individual school was unlikely to have a host of policies covering every aspect of that school's work. Job descriptions were relatively new and were, in my case, summed up in the phrase "Teacher of Chemistry". Apart from a teacher's probationary year there was no systematic appraisal process, still less the formal target setting that characterises performance management. A school could set out its own curriculum within the framework provided by the Local Education Authority. The examination system was essentially defined by the Certificate of Secondary Education (offering examinations at 16) and the General Certificate of Education offering examinations at 16 (Ordinary level) and at 18 (Advanced level). An individual school and indeed an individual teacher had far greater power to innovate and to work to meet the needs of the children as they saw them. In 1976 I was required to ensure that my pupils reached a certain point at the end of each year ready for an end of year examination set by the department. As a science teacher, the only limitation on my planning was the availability of equipment and it was the task of the Head of Department to manage that. The picture today, with a diversity of provision, a culture of accountability and an ever changing set of expectations placed on schools, is very different.

It is a truism that the last thirty years have also seen very rapid changes in communications technology and information technology.

THE HEAD SPEAKS

The original prediction of Gordon Moore, later known as Moore's Law, was that the number of transistors that can be placed in an integrated circuit doubles every two years. Moore's prediction, stated in 1965, has proved to be the case for over forty years. The effect has been to make devices become ever smaller and increasingly powerful. Few will have foreseen, however, the profound effect of these devices on society. The development of the internet and networks capable of transmitting massive amounts of data has given large sections of the population access to quantities of information that previously would have been available to very few. Not surprisingly schools have had to respond to the new technology, though progress has been relatively slow compared to the rest of society. This is perhaps because schools were traditionally seen by society, and a good number of teachers, as places where information and knowledge are dispensed, not as places where pupils learn how to gain knowledge for themselves.

In the 1970s, computers in schools were rare. Computing networks, which existed at universities, were almost unknown in schools. Relatively few people had any experience of either computing or still less programming. I programmed my first computer in 1969 (using punched tape) while working in industry. Throughout my time at university I was in one way or another using the, even then, rapidly developing computer systems available in universities. By the end of the 1970s my school had acquired the first 380z PC computer which was followed by a few others. I programmed this machine to be of some help with the timetabling process and was aware that some pupils were starting to acquire the home versions of these machines. The computers were, however, the property of the Maths department though they were beginning to be used to help support school administration, particularly the timetable. In the Chemistry department of that school, we experimented with a Texas programmable calculator so that students could check some of their calculations from experiments. We also used the device to produce simple pH curves as a way of reinforcing that area of the curriculum.

My second school was somewhat further down the ICT road. At this independent school the BBC microcomputer was being used but the machines were networked and linked to a server. For the first time, I saw children learning computing skills. A variety of software for use on these computers was also starting to appear. In addition to the networked machines, a computer on a trolley was used in the laboratories to support some classroom teaching. A number of these programmes were simulations which allowed the teacher to demonstrate quickly the effect of changing variables. Though I did not at that time have any role in school administration, it seemed to me that using computers in this area was likely to be a very fruitful path to explore. For most teachers, however, computers were a poor alternative to the new VCR machines which started to appear in the late 1970s.

Despite the unrest of the late eighties, teachers were making significant changes to their practice and exploring the potential of the rapidly improving computers that were becoming available. Computers in the form of the BBC micro (first released in 1981), the ZX Spectrum (first released in 1982), the Atari (which began producing home computers in the 1970s) and others were in homes as games platforms. The use of the spreadsheet and word processor were growing but these had relatively little impact on teaching styles or on teaching practice. Part of the problem was a dearth of good quality educational software. What was available was poor in comparison to games software. Educational computing was usually seen in Common Rooms as the province of "techies" like me. Computing systems were at that time unreliable and potential users were at the mercy of a system that would fail in the middle of a lesson. Storage was limited but growing rapidly as hard drives started to come on the market.

Government recognition of the very rapid growth in Information Technology in commerce and industry required schools to ensure that children were made aware of these changes. Initiatives such as the Technical and Vocational Education Initiative (TVEI) were used by some LEAs as a way of supporting the growth of ICT in schools. It could often be the case that the young pupil enthusiast for IT would have significantly more knowledge of computing than many of his or her teachers. This did little to increase the confidence of teachers who were considering using computers. Nevertheless I became convinced that computers could make a contribution to teaching, but that such a use required more stable systems and the use of networks.

Moving to Bristol Grammar School I found myself in an excellent school that had made little movement toward the new technology but was ready to make such a move. Part of my new responsibilities was to support and manage this move. Against the then prevailing orthodoxy I believed that the future for educational computing had to be based on the dominant systems with large user bases. For this reason the operating system had to be that provided by Microsoft despite what I saw as significant weaknesses – in particular the need to use system based commands instead of more intuitive icon based systems such as existed on the Atari or Mac systems.

As a result, all the school office typewriters were replaced by computers and staff trained to use word processing and spreadsheet software. A timetabling package was introduced and used to construct the timetable in 1990, replacing the previous paper based system. This change in itself allowed the school to adopt a much more flexible curriculum. Prior to 1990, little flexibility was available because of the difficulty of tracking the various choices of students. Using a computer system allowed us to ensure that the timetable was simply the servant of our curriculum and that it reflected the choices of students. At the same time the now ageing BBC microcomputers were replaced by RM PC machines, though the BBC machines continued to be useful in the science department. A small database system was written to generate lists and this started our consideration of what we wanted from a school information management system. Bristol Grammar School was among the first group of independent schools to introduce a school information management system. The small computer networks of the early nineties installed in strategic parts of the school were replaced by the mid-nineties with an extensive fibre-optic network connecting all parts of the school. Exam results began to be streamed into the school via a modem. E-mail started to replace paper as the means of communication as the network grew and managers at all levels used the school database as a matter of routine. More recently reports to parents were compiled through a web-based system which allows teachers to write their comments from anywhere in the world. At some point in this period we stopped talking about

Information Technology and started referring to Information and Communication Technology. ICT technical support grew significantly from a part-time post to a systems manager supported by three technicians.

Developing the use of ICT in the classroom has been significantly slower. At any one time determining the appropriate skills for pupils has been relatively simple but finding an appropriate qualification to accredit these skills has been far from straightforward. Early versions of IT skills courses usually took their lead from computing courses, which tended to place an overemphasis on system architecture and programming. Whatever the course, however, the ICT infrastructure had to be capable of supporting the demand generated by the users of the system. In our early efforts to build systems this was not always achieved. Today, for an effective level of ICT capability a school needs well structured and robust systems that have sufficient bandwidth to allow rapid connection to a range of data sources. Constructing such a network demands both a detailed analysis of the school's current needs and also an anticipation of the possible growth. It requires skills and understanding that are often not present in schools.

Our ICT strategy was based on a simple idea: that ICT resources in the school should be available, as they are for almost all other users of ICT, when and where the pupil wants them. This led us to move to radio networks across the school supported by our fibre-optic core. As a first application of this idea banks of laptops in the library, in the junior school and in departmental areas offer ICT services as needed. In order to support the use of ICT by teachers we have provided all teachers with laptops, many of which have tablet functionality (i.e. they have touch sensitive screens and pens). This is further supported by data projectors in every classroom and interactive white boards in some classrooms. Developments of this sort are certainly not unique to my school. The new costs associated with ICT have become a significant part of the budgets of all schools, yet it could be argued that the slowness of uptake of ICT in schools has been conditioned by the limitations of the funding that was and is available.

The introduction of powerful ICT infrastructures into schools does not, of itself, improve teaching or learning. There is always a danger that schools become fixated on the technology itself. ICT infrastructure in the modern world is no more exceptional than the provision of facilities for Sport, Mathematics, Science or any of the many activities that schools provide. In educational terms schools must consider the opportunities for teaching and learning offered by this new technology, how to give children an understanding of the implications of the new technology for society and what skills children need to have in order to be autonomous users of the technology both now and as it evolves.

The use of ICT in a given class or subject area should always be justified in pedagogic terms. I did not and do not believe that demonstration of ICT capability should force the adoption of ICT based techniques. Early visions of the use of ICT tended to focus on specific ICT tools such as word-processing, spreadsheets and databases, with a view that use of these was to demonstrate ICT capability. The danger of this is to produce closed activities whose purpose relates only marginally to the subject area and focuses on a particular ICT skill. The use of spreadsheets in Mathematics is a powerful tool in appropriate contexts but should be seen as supporting the development of mathematical skills. Skills in word-processing are, in my view, currently essential for a student of the twenty-first century but these in themselves do not necessarily support, for example, the learning of English. Inevitably this means that progress in the use of classroom ICT by a given subject area will vary from subject to subject and will change with the technology.

The growth of network devices and techniques such as social networks, blogs, RSS feeds and podcasts offers a new range of potential tools for teachers to use. The emergence of e-portals and Virtual Learning Environments allows the activities of the school to link with home. The work of Alan November and the November Learning website give examples of what can be done. For example in English departments, it is easy to see that VCR can be replaced by a multimedia device linked to a data projector or plasma screen. Such a system can draw on a multimedia server allowing a number of sources to be used simultaneously. This is simply the use of a more effective piece of technology to replace another and does not constitute a significant use of ICT capability, except perhaps in that the teacher must understand how to turn the system on. A blog may prove to be a useful way of teaching some aspects of writing or could serve as a useful way of preparing for a classroom discussion. This latter application allows all members of the class to contribute and for their contributions to be seen by all members of the class. The blog need not be public, but confined to the group of learners with the blog linking to a class teacher. These new opportunities simply give the skilled teacher a greater range of strategies that can be deployed and that have the advantage of relating to the way that young people are using the technology themselves. Techniques such as those described will not, in my view, replace other well tried methods.

The development of school information systems has allowed schools to collect large amounts of data that relate to the progress of pupils. The possession of such data does not support teaching and learning unless it is used to measure progress. One of the new "value-added" systems, such as those provided by the CEM centre, allows schools to look at the progress of their pupils in an objective way, particularly when the external data provided by sources like CEM is combined with a school's internal data from its own testing. Professor Carol Fitzgibbon once referred to the use of such data as "measurement without malice" in contradistinction to much of the league table data generated by the national press and government.

Such is the pace of development that it would now be difficult to find significant parts of society that are not in some way dependent on ICT. The speed of change has left schools struggling to determine what they should do in curriculum terms to respond. Not surprisingly, installing the technology has to date been a major part of that response. Much ICT teaching is skills-based and pays relatively little attention to the implications of the technology. There is general agreement that ICT must be given due attention in the curriculum but it is difficult to find clarity as to what the nature of that attention should be. The National College for School Leadership describes the school of the future as an e-confident school – presumably then full of e-confident learners and teachers. 2020 Vision describes a school in which 'Using

ICT will be natural for most pupils and for an increasing majority of teachers'. 2020 Vision assumes that 'access to personal, multifunctional devices' together with access to 'increasing amounts of information' will be a characteristic of schools in 2020. Personalised learning is also predicted to be a key component of learning in 2020. The assessment and accreditation of such a system call for large database structures such as those that are being developed by the examination boards. The development of these structures is not easy as recent experience of such developments shows. Individual head teachers will need to continue to be pragmatic about adopting such schemes.

It is difficult and almost certainly unwise to predict where ICT could take schools over the next few years. Should all children in a school have their own laptop or personal multi-functional device as Vision 2020 suggests? In the developing world the 'one laptop per child' initiative intends to ensure that every child in the developing world has access to ICT. This is leading to the development of devices with low power requirements that can operate in demanding environments. Such devices may well be of interest to schools in this country. Children already carry powerful devices in their pockets and bags in the form of mobile phones, some of which will be capable of internet access, have the functions of a personal data assistant and also act as mp3 players. I believe that that the use of some form of personal data device will be in regular use in schools within the next decade. The management of such devices will present schools with further challenges. Surfing the internet can be a powerful way of searching for information quickly but it can equally act as 'visual heroin', becoming a distraction to learning. Schools will need to consider how to construct systems which constrain such activity or educate their users in appropriate research techniques. Today's young people are multi-tasking in a way that is unfamiliar to their parents but will be a given in the schools of the future.

Learning to interact with information systems in an effective way will be an important part of the education of the future. People will need to know how to use search engines effectively and how to judge the quality of information that they find. New tools are emerging that allow searches to be more effective: *Google Scholar* provides a simple way to search broadly for scholarly literature, and *Intute* provides access to web resources for education and research that have been evaluated by subject specialists. Sources such as *Wikipedia* may offer authoritative guidance on a particular topic but there is no way, currently, of determining this without cross checking with other sources. Students must possess both the skills to use such information systems and understand the value and limitations of the information they obtain. New libraries will give access to the more fluid sources of information such as *Wikipedia*, online reference resources of the type currently represented by *Encyclopaedia Britannica Online* and *JSTOR* (an online journal archive), newspapers, periodicals and, of course, books. The informed user of data will understand how to cross-reference all these sources effectively. In marked contrast to learning in schools prior to the introduction of ICT systems, meta-knowledge will be a significant part of children's learning.

Some students will want the technical training that will enable them to become the architects of future systems but the majority will be users of information services either directly or indirectly. Current orthodoxy puts little emphasis on a basic understanding of programming, yet the problem solving skills that such an understanding gives are capable of wide application. Other countries do not seem to take the same view of programming skills. The same could be said of the great advances in graphics processing. All of us have now experienced the effect of this as digital photography has replaced film with flash drive. The techniques that allow significant and almost undetectable changes to any image and the construction of virtual environments that are barely distinguishable from the real thing give rise to the need for the young people of tomorrow to understand both the techniques and the implications of these technologies.

It is time that information technology became part of the experience of every child. All children should have ICT skills, an understanding of information systems and an understanding of the implications of information systems for society. They should understand the nature of network communities and the means of participating in such communities will be a part of that understanding. They should see ICT being used effectively by teachers and they will use their own ICT skills to support their work. They should be confident and creative users of the technology. If we do not ensure this we risk the next generation not only being as ill-prepared for a rapidly changing environment as perhaps we were but also that they will be ill-equipped for life in an increasingly global marketplace for skills.

Author's Note

I have to thank Denise Brooks, Robert Gullifer, Paul Roberts and Nick Hammond for helpful suggestions and for proof reading this article. The errors and omissions are however entirely my own but I have made use of a large number of websites for factual information. The most significant of these are listed below:

About Google Scholar. (n.d.). Retrieved January 2008, from Google Scholar: http://scholar.google.co.uk/intl/en/scholar/about.html

About Intute. (n.d.). Retrieved January 21, 2008, from Intute: http://www.intute.ac.uk/about.html

Contact Point. (n.d.). Retrieved January 10, 2008, from Every Child Matters:

http://www.everychildmatters.gov.uk/deliveringservices/contactpoint/

History. (n.d.). Retrieved January 9, 2008, from Derek Gillard's Website: http://www.dg.dial.pipex.com/index.shtml

Home. (n.d.). Retrieved January 21, 2008, from Britannica Online: http://info.britannica.co.uk/

Mission. (n.d.). Retrieved January 21, 2008, from JSTOR - The Scholarly Journal Archive: http://www.jstor.org/about/mission.html

November Learning. (n.d.). Retrieved January 3, 2008, from November Learning: http://novemberlearning.com/index.php

One Laptop per Child. (n.d.). Retrieved January 8, 2008, from One Laptop per Child: http://laptop.org/

SIMS. (n.d.). Retrieved January 10, 2008, from Capita Education Services: http://www.capitaes.co.uk/SIMS/index.asp

Teachernet. (n.d.). Retrieved January 3, 2008, from Teachernet: http://www.teachernet.gov.uk/

The CEM centre. (n.d.). Retrieved January 11, 2008, from The CEM Centre: http://www.cemcentre.org/

Towards the e-confident school. (n.d.). Retrieved January 10, 2008, from Becta:

http://www.becta.org.uk/page_documents/leaders/governors/e-confident.pdf

Wikipedia. (n.d.). Retrieved January 10, 2008, from Wikipedia: http://en.wikipedia.org/wiki/Main_Page

THE GLASGOW ACADEMY

'A PLEA FOR MODERNITY' (1936)

F. Roydon Richards

In 1936, F. Roydon Richards makes 'A Plea for Modernity', confessing that, 'A Head Master's work leaves scanty time for reflecting on fundamental principles':

Even if his responsibilities do not involve the charge of his pupils for the whole round of the clock, there are sufficient problems to compel him to live from one minor crisis to the next. Here, for example, are some taken at random: numbers, staffing, finance, organization, time-tables, discipline, interviews, syllabuses, examinations, correspondence, co-ordination, inspection, and, by way of relaxation, a little teaching.

So the mound of paperwork on a Head's desk is nothing new!

Writing at a time of 'perpetual reports of international tension ..... when the education of whole masses is perverted to suit the doctrines of the totalitarian state', Richards argues the importance of laying the foundations of international respect and co-operation during the years of schooling. There must, he believes, be far more of a focus on politics – something that might be best taught in History – and 'if citizenship is to be taken seriously, then History and its dependent activities have the strongest of claims to encroach on the more venerable disciplines'. For the same reason he also proposes an increase in the time given to Modern Languages, lamenting the fact that 'grammatical accuracy ..... ranks so highly among the scholastic virtues', forcing the language master to minimize or even exclude from his lessons 'topics most pertinent to culture' because of the demands of the examination syllabus.

Richards goes on to argue that teaching religion – which has become 'anaemic.... as a moral and social force' – is more important than ever, but that fewer and fewer recruits to the teaching profession have the commitment to teach it. He wants to see greater emphasis on Art and the development of 'taste', not least because 'much ugliness has to be tolerated in modern life because aesthetic considerations are overridden by financial'. Music, too, is an essential part of a liberal education.

The trouble for Richards is that too much emphasis is put on the School Certificate by parents and employer so no Head can risk taking time away from examination subjects in order to broaden the curriculum. But for pupils whose strengths are not academic, a programme founded on citizenship, religion, aesthetic culture and contact with reality would be far more appropriate – with more time given to the qualitative rather than the quantitative aspects of Science, to foreign Geography and Culture rather than to Modern Languages, and to reading for pleasure and experience rather than for examination cramming.

Few, of course, have ever listened for long to such good sense. In our utilitarian world, academic achievement has become a social necessity, fuelled by a culture of league tables, and whatever governments and schools do or say, vocational qualifications have somehow become little more than badges of shame.

LIGHTING FIRES: CAN DO/WILL DO, THE SMALL 'I' AND THE BIG 'WE'

Peter Brodie

Education is not the filling of a pail, but the lighting of a fire. Yeats was right about that. Schools can indeed change children's lives, and inspirational teachers, of whom there are many, do this by infectious passion for their subject and by commitment to their pupils. They communicate to their pupils that they believe in them and thereby enable them to believe in themselves. That encourages the purposeful engagement necessary to excel. These teachers set the highest of challenges and standards, and show children how to attain them, praising both effort and good strategies. They nurture children and ensure that they are always clear on their next steps. So the children see what they can do and are helped to have a plan and vision of themselves doing it. Above all, inspirational teachers switch on children's can-do, will-do mindset: the keenness to learn and the sense of self-efficacy which are so important to success. You can see the connections being made in the classroom, and that is why I cannot envisage appointing a teacher without first watching him or her teach.

Churchill said, but I doubt many would now agree – great man though he was – that 'Headmasters have powers at their disposal with which Prime Ministers have never yet been invested'. The media regale us with a catalogue of family and social breakdown, the hedonistic treadmill of instant gratification (rather than the deferred gratification on which education depends), materialism, narcissism, peer pressure, substance abuse, the rise of relativism and rights, the rejection of responsibilities, authority and values, the commercialisation of childhood, the cult of celebrity, the fragmentation of a shared culture, and the growing health issues related to rising obesity and emotional health. The UK's children appear the most unhappy in the developed world, and some of that unhappiness centres on the self being put before others. So the task of educators is to create a lifelong love of learning and help the big 'I' and small 'we' develop into the big 'we' and a more deeply fulfilled 'I'. Excellence is our passion, and our challenge is to do the very best we can for all the children we teach so that they develop into rounded and fulfilled young people who care about others.

Schools' values can be constants in some children's lives of change. Teachers' belief in them and devoted support of them can be the rock they need. Whatever the difficulties, it is both the greatest and most satisfying of educational challenges to endeavour to enable every child to develop the optimum learning mindset and become an autonomous lifelong learner. Eastern cultures tend to value perseverance more than our own, and their high educational achievement is not unconnected with that. Our children and teachers need to live out the belief that intelligence and abilities are not fixed, that our brains are constantly building new connections, and that every experience and relationship throughout our lives is an opportunity for learning. Central to this is recognition of the value – and fun – of engaging in a shared enterprise in a spirit of mutual support, openness and trust. Many children already have the right mindset, but the key for those who don't is switching out of one which unhelpfully judges or fears judgement. That mindset only repeats patterns from the past and short circuits learning. We have to help children feel that mistakes are often the best way to learn, and the only failure is not being ready to learn from them. If we can accomplish this, we have put them in charge of their minds and learning. The shift must be made into openness to the excitement of learning and to the pleasure of mastering an area, as well as recognition that the truly worthwhile requires effort and resilience. If success takes time, that simply emphasises the need to use all available strategies to the full and work at it. The challenge is to ensure that every child develops this learning mindset and then makes the utmost of the rich opportunities in our schools. If they can do that, they should be confident, flexible, rounded and entrepreneurial lifelong learners, and more likely to enjoy the positive relationships and fulfilled lives contributing to society that we would wish for them. They will have experienced the value of 'we' rather than 'I' and be readier to express concern for others in their own lives rather than being locked in the self.

Many schools have developed admirably extensive study skills programmes. As a result of them, most children can say what it is that they should be doing. The problem is that not all children do it. So motivation really matters, and we must do all we can to cater for the individual. I have found two books very useful on this key area of motivational mindsets: Alan McLean's *The Motivated School* and Carol S. Dweck's *Mindset*. McLean stresses the importance of developing in our children a sense of self-efficacy through a positive culture of care and engagement, stimulation, enjoyment and feedback. Dweck explores numerous strategies for developing mindsets for growth. In recounting research on groups of children given study skills training, she contrasts the success of children who were also inspired to take control of their minds against the relative lack of success of those who simply had more study skills training. You are left in no doubt that our mission should be to help children take control of their minds, and thereby become leaders of their own learning.

This is why strong pastoral or personal support systems are central to success. Children benefit from having their own dedicated adult personal supporter (or 'tutor') who cares for them throughout their time in the school. It is even better if he or she has no more than a dozen children to care for: if all teachers are tutors, caring is truly at the centre of the school and the people who enrich children's lives by caring are the same as those who do so by teaching. The roles complement each other and it is important that the adults with whom children come into contact embody these doubly nurturing roles. If tutor and tutee have daily contact with each other, plus a longer session or tutor period each week, they will know each other well and issues can be resolved promptly and with a lightness of touch.

Tutors' achievements can be considerable. They can encourage children and help them appreciate their own achievements, talk children through challenges and solutions, enable them to feel that effort generates improvement, find and reinforce successful strategies, praise effort, help children think for themselves, aid self-evaluation, plan and set smart targets, nurture potential through high but realistic expectations, and enable them to visualise themselves succeeding. Good tutors raise and share tutees' aspirations. They enhance their sense of self-efficacy and sense of the possible and desirable. They can give tutees the encouragement sometimes needed to stand apart from a friend or peer pressure and go for what is best for their future. They also look for and nurture talents, and ensure that children are making the most of all the opportunities for support around the school, be they subject clinics, revision sessions or using the open door policy of staff who are ready to see anyone who will benefit from help.

Good tutors keep parents informed and seek their support whenever appropriate. Gifted tutors know how to have skilful conversations that encourage tutees to engage with clubs, societies and trips: they know how to charm perhaps reluctant adolescents into activities which, despite initial resistance, they come to love. Sometimes they set this up carefully, getting colleagues on side in advance or priming them with appropriate background and responses. There are few things more rewarding than seeing someone's life blossom because of an activity their tutor or Head of House enabled him or her to be involved in. So the role of the tutor is harnessing the power of the possible, firing the child's imagination and visualization of achievement, and nurturing effort, standards and accomplishment. If there is a highly effective vertical House structure, there is the added benefit of a child having at least two adults who will know him or her really well throughout the school, and the possibility if one is having to take a very firm line of the other being clearly felt still to be a gentler 'friend' despite all. The tutor and House system are powerful ways of showing children they belong, are valued, respected and trusted, and can achieve. They are also excellent ways of providing children with responsibilities and opportunities for decision making and sharing their lives with others.

We can give our children few greater gifts than to experience in school how to make good things happen for themselves and others. It is a valuable lesson early on to learn how to run with a good idea and make a success of it whatever barriers stand in the way. I believe it is important to give children that experience as often and as fully as we can. It builds confidence, creativity and flexibility, it moves them from 'I' to 'we', and it can transform how they see themselves and school. A sense of self-efficacy in one area spreads to others. We are preparing our children for a world where many will have a series of jobs in careers which as yet do not exist. They will face serious competition from societies which value education far more, combining higher performance in international tests with an emphasis on rigorous endeavour and self-improvement, greater social discipline and an absence of self-indulgent individualism or (as some put it) Western decadence. We know that the future of First World countries will belong increasingly to the creative industries – or to creative thinkers and doers in other areas. It will belong especially to creative work at and beyond the edges of subject boundaries, which are likely to become increasingly blurred. Yet in the pursuit of creativity and skills we must not lose sight of the value of the discipline of acquiring knowledge, and the discipline of knowing and judging what is valuable or relevant knowledge, and how best to develop and use it for a moral purpose.

THE HEAD SPEAKS

Our children's future requires a can-do, will-do attitude, where intelligence is applied creatively, diligently and responsibly to generate solutions which benefit themselves and others. So our schools need to do all they can to develop that can-do, will-do enterprising spirit now, and to give practice in the values and judgements which should guide it. It is vital to encourage children's initiative, enterprise and responsibility. Our schools can help children seize the future by ensuring that they themselves create and develop opportunities in the present.

We know that we all learn best when there is a real motivation to learn and a realistic context in which to do so. Education has most impact when it is most realistic. So it makes sense to create opportunities for children to take responsibility for their learning and discover the satisfactions of working with others in enterprises which reflect realities and carry through to productive outcomes with genuine impact. An enormous strength of British schools is the many sporting, artistic, cultural, intellectual, outdoor and social opportunities they have long provided. These are fundamental in enabling children to engage, discover the disciplines and satisfactions of teamwork, and stretch themselves. Team games provide important opportunities to lead, or be valuable team members working for the common good, to develop decision making skills and to experience the benefits of 'we' rather than 'I'. In the broader context of a mutually supportive ethos, properly managed competition in sport or any other activity, not least debating, enables children to learn to handle successes and failures. Sport or music tours create exciting challenges and develop children's confidence and understanding of the world. Charity fundraising, helping less privileged children in the UK or overseas, or working on environmental projects, are all valuable activities which also reinforce academic potential.

There are many ways of developing children's initiative, leadership and responsibility. One is encouraging pupil-produced (and ideally pupil-written) dramatic and musical productions and presentations. Saying to the whole school that it should be them, not the Head, on the stage can liberate a wealth of talent and drive. It is remarkable how children can rise to the responsibility of working with and directing their peers, how much they learn in the process and how good the growth makes them feel about themselves. They may well come up with a production you would never have contemplated and carry it off with unexpected flair. Recently my school has enjoyed, amongst other productions and presentations, pupil-directed versions of *The Sound of Music*, *Animal Farm*, a pupil-written, pupil-choreographed pantomime, and *An Inspector Calls*, with a director aged fourteen and a cast of twelve, thirteen and fourteen year olds. The pupil directors and organisers develop skills in negotiation, diplomacy, time management and project management, and experience real responsibility in handling not just their peers but also members of staff responsible for PR, lighting and sound, make-up, set-building, front of house, catering, the calendar, bookings, finance, the janitors and so on. Producing flyers, posters and programmes teaches much about presentational techniques, and taking the bookings and money and sending out the tickets breeds accountability. Schools sometimes present significant barriers to mounting productions, not least restricted rehearsal time because of other activities putting constraints on children's time or performance space. Overcoming these barriers develops real skills of empathy and communication, and often of very committed but still tactful persuasion. Coping with difficulties or setbacks enhances patience and resilience. Children learn when and how to make and communicate decisions, and when to take a stand, whether it be at auditions, insisting on lines being learned (and handling the fall-out when they are not), or over an interpretation or technical detail. Above all, they will learn a great deal about producing a quality product to a deadline. Discipline, rigour and standards are at the heart of successful creativity, and children will have learnt that.

It may be that the producers or directors are younger or very different from their cast or technical crews, in which case they are also learning how to communicate despite difference. Most importantly, older pupils working cooperatively with younger pupils communicate one of the most important things any good school can: that responsible individuals care about others, that it is right and proper that members of communities give to others across differences of age or background, and that pupils set examples for others to follow. We should never underestimate the power of role models. Nor should we cease seeking ways to use them for good.

Of course, things can go wrong. Disasters can be avoided by a short checklist of members of staff to liaise with, covering everything from acquiring performance rights to the appropriate presence of responsible adults, one of whom can drop in supportively and with a lightness of touch on the odd rehearsal to establish that all is on track. The benefits are enormous because in schools what happens one year becomes a tradition the next. That way, children hand on initiative, successful endeavour and standards to those who follow them.

Our responsibility to extend and challenge the young people in our care makes Outdoor Education a key area. It offers youngsters very special challenges, including the chance to overcome psychologically demanding situations. It teaches them about risk management and does not rely on academic, artistic or sporting prowess: those who lack physical coordination or are not fond of traditional sports can find it deeply rewarding. As my Head of Outdoor Education points out, Outdoor Education can provide life-enduring memories because the situations are so different from most individuals' norm. Even someone susceptible to the teenage world of bravado can feel humbled by the enormousness and power of the natural environment. It is far bigger and more significant than they will ever be, and they observe, occasionally very closely, that their bodies are not immortal.

On a pioneering Glasgow Academy expedition to the Arctic, our pupils scaled an unclimbed peak in East Greenland, thereby earning the right to name it. Without adults, they scaled another peak which had only been climbed once before, at a different time of year, by adult mountaineers. They devoted months of demanding and thorough preparation to these adventures, which were powerful and enriching experiences that changed them. As they said:

We now felt as if we were real mountaineers.... It makes you realise how little you need to be happy. I've never been so content in my life.

THE HEAD SPEAKS

Education is best when we equip children with knowledge and skills, and then have the courage to allow them to use them. We should seek occasions that allow children to feel that they have done what adults do, that they are trusted, and that they have proved themselves. It is all the better if teachers are participating in activities on an equal footing to the pupils, as they often can be in Outdoor Education. Giving to children outside the classroom brings manifold rewards within the classroom too.

Cooperative learning, team working, peer assessment, networking and enterprise are of growing importance in schools. Many schools have successful 'buddy' schemes, and pupils mentoring pupils is a further way of developing a culture of learning, responsibility and care for others. It may involve senior students giving younger children one-to-one conversation practice in Modern Languages classrooms, helping them get to grips with a mathematical concept that needs just a little more practice, or giving support for learning to those who benefit from it in any other subject. It may involve older students helping out with sports. Or perhaps senior students can discuss work and other issues with younger children at tutor registration times or in tutor periods, or give presentations to House or School assemblies. Children with difficulties can be paired with older students who have surmounted those difficulties, or who have found successful ways of working in whatever area is proving a challenge.

Schools require spaces which encourage such new ways of learning to happen. School buildings need to be welcoming, inspirational and iconic places expressing the school's values. They should communicate its vision of a stimulating learning community, embody its aspirational ethos and be designed to provide future-proofed flexibility and freedom for children and staff to do what they want to do. The motivational effects of good design on children and staff are enormous. The challenge is to maximise the way buildings transmit learning and provide a whole variety of teaching opportunities, gaining maximum learning from every area, including circulation areas. Corridors are increasingly replaced by airy and light public places for ad hoc creativity, learning and teaching, and meeting points where students, staff and visitors delight in being. These should be places where all feel at home sharing ideas, knowledge and skills, and where students' work of all kinds (and why not staff's alongside?) can be displayed. Buildings should celebrate the community's achievements, embodying its pride and joy. There is enormous power in photos displayed around them of happy children and staff engaging in multifarious activities: they say to new pupils and parents, 'This is what we do. This can be your future too'.

Given the growing informality of modern culture, our awareness of the power of individuals' interactions, and the importance of satisfying social needs, these new spaces should be social spaces too: social spaces top most children's wish lists (along with quality toilet facilities). We know our greatest resources are our people – colleagues, children and the community. If we provide comfortable and flexible new spaces for them, new interactions and new relationships between different disciplines and kinds of learning will occur. Full consultation and collaboration from the very start with all who will use them makes them better places and strengthens the school culture: children and staff will see needs, problems and solutions others may not.

Classrooms need to be big enough not to be forced to have desks in rows, and to enable work in groups of varying sizes, experiential learning, easy access to resources and, of course, plenty of storage space. They are becoming more like studios zoned for different activities. Temperature and ventilation should be controllable in each room, lockers large, and corridors – if they must exist – broad or acting as break-out zones, with thought given to how their walls and floors can generate learning: they might compensate for gaps in children's culture by timelines running along them displaying significant global, national or local achievements, events or geographical knowledge. On the way to a science area you could follow or be surrounded by scientific discoveries, or have the periodic table on the floor, which might also conveniently show where to replace furniture after activities. The building itself can teach, not least through exemplification and explanation of environmental credentials: its passive design, use of daylight, natural ventilation, natural healthy materials and finishes, and sustainability. Full spectrum light has been found to raise mood, focus, attainment and attendance, whilst sensitive use of colour and materials can develop children's aesthetic sense. Finally, of course, inspirational buildings should sit well in their setting, ideally sensitively landscaped in ways that provide a wide variety of outdoor challenges and experiences for the children, along with seating and shelter. There is a lot in the saying that every child has three teachers: the other children, the teacher and the space.

Our buildings can communicate the adventure of learning, but we need also to harness the motivational effects of advancing technology. These new spaces should enable the 'learn anywhere, anytime' culture that grows as ICT is embedded in the life of the community. They should also facilitate the new literacies and opportunities for children to make choices about their learning, for we know that choice enhances learning. The goal of enabling children to take responsibility for their learning becomes more achievable by promoting use of technology which enables individualised learning. Virtual learning environments such as *Scholar* or BBC *Bitesize* have much to offer. Every generation in the modern world has faced technological change: the challenge as it moves ever faster, and with ever greater financial implications, is to ensure that it provides genuinely enhanced learning and creates connectivity rather than insularity.

Schools have a duty shared with parents/carers to enable children to become confident individuals, successful learners, effective contributors and responsible citizens – the declared outcomes of the Scottish Curriculum for Excellence. These have long been goals of good schools, implicitly or explicitly, and the Curriculum for Excellence sits well with the traditional strengths of independent schools in developing rounded excellence. International research tells us that young people who have good communication with their mother and/or father are less likely to report unhappy lives, poor health, smoking or drunkenness than their peers who have poor communication with parents. Children often need time to talk, time to listen, time to feel valued and time to love and be loved – not an increase in possessions, which are no compensation for emotional neglect. A great deal can be achieved at home by responsible caring parenting and there is much to recommend our young people being given the best possible preparation for parenthood, and appreciating particularly the benefits of parents who read books with their children, stimulate them, talk through the day and share aspirations and standards with them.

Partnership between parents and schools is central to raising attainment. However, not every child has parents, carers or siblings who ask, 'What did you learn today? What strategies did you use? What feedback did you get? What do you want to achieve tomorrow? How will you go about that? Can we do anything to help?' Nor may every child hear much sharing of experiences of perseverance in overcoming difficulties. So where there is limited family exchange of experiences over the evening meal, whilst travelling, or whatever, it is all the more important that schools have dynamic pastoral and personal support systems with tutors passionate about engaging children in these conversations. That way, children can reflect on their learning and share the wisdom of their own and others' experience.

The techniques of conflict resolution used in Restorative Justice are another important means of modelling the responsible and mutually supportive culture we wish children and staff to enjoy in school and carry through life. They enable people to feel listened to and to recognise that listening to others, accepting responsibility, making amends and thinking about and expressing clearly what matters is the way ahead.

Behind all the above lie two key beliefs: belief in the power of an enterprising can do, will do culture, together with belief in the liberation of abilities of all kinds through an ethos of initiative, trust and positive feedback. There is great value in engaging and empowering those presently – or potentially – abler than oneself. G. K. Chesterton's definition of education as '… the soul of a society as it passes from one generation to another' sums up the transmission of collective spirit and wisdom, but education is also what is left when you have forgotten what has been learnt. It is how our young people will live their lives after they have left our care that should guide us above all. The development of character and values, and the liberation of talents and creativities of all kinds, have long been important in British schools. Time is too fleeting for our children not to live lives fruitfully to the best of their ability. If we develop their readiness to learn, their initiative, team work and responsibility, they will appreciate – despite all the pressures of materialism – that the best things in life are not things. For me, that is the ultimate moral purpose of teaching and headship. We have only one chance with the education of our children, so their tomorrow must be our urgency today – in a school filled with laughter and a sense of fun.

THE MANCHESTER GRAMMAR SCHOOL

'THE SCHOOL AND THE COMMUNITY' (1936)

Douglas Miller

Douglas Miller begins by complaining of the neglect in the secondary school of manual craft, widening his argument to suggest that 'the true test of a subject's value is not its immediate usefulness for a boy's vocation, but its power to develop in the fullest sense his personality'. While also arguing the importance of making boys aware of their heritage, the Parliamentary system and local government, he nevertheless believes that 'our first duty is to teach our subjects, apart from time and place, to kindle in the hearts of youth the true love of learning, the appreciation of the best that has been taught and done'.

In 1936, as today, there were complaints that Sixth Form study had become too specialized. But Miller rebuts the complaints:

We are all agreed that a narrow pedantic course of study at the age of sixteen to eighteen is wrong. What we do not admit is that you gain breadth by merely increasing the number of subjects studied. Breadth depends on the manner in which a subject is approached, and it is possible to study a large variety of subjects without achieving any understanding of their essential significance.

Miller notes the growth in the day Public Schools of extra-curricular activities, including camping and trekking abroad; the greater latitude enjoyed by boys ('It has its dangers, but on the balance schoolmasters would agree that the atmosphere is healthier for the change'); and the fact that 'the relationship between boy and master has become sound and sane'. He defends homework, not least because it 'keeps home in touch with the efforts of school'; and, as the storm clouds of war gather and threaten, he defends boys accused of being less 'virile' than the previous generation and of having an apparently pacifist attitude ('We schoolmasters know that beneath the careless exterior lies the same capacity for sacrifice').

Finally, in arguing for the school-leaving age [which stood at fourteen] to be raised, he worries that, 'It is the boy of ordinary intelligence that now needs our care'. Bright boys from the humblest origins can climb the educational ladder to the highest posts in the land; but it is the right of all to benefit from secondary education, whatever the demands of industry for 'junior' employees.

THE RETREAT FROM SCHOLARSHIP

Christopher Ray

We look to scholarship to stimulate new thinking and research, to sharpen our reflections upon existing thought, and to instil a sense of excitement about the life of the intellect. We look to scholars for intellectual leadership and inspiration.

It is not easy to provide a definition of scholarship which is both concise and satisfactory: it is less of a problem to identify those whom we are willing to accept as scholars of significance. John Stuart Mill was arguably one of the finest academics of the nineteenth century and might be regarded as an exemplar of a scholar. A profound thinker and prolific writer, he produced immensely influential works such as *Utilitarianism*, *On Liberty*, and *System of Logic*. Other fine scholars of that period undoubtedly include Jeremy Bentham (Jurisprudence), Charles Darwin (Biology), and Benjamin Jowett (Classics). The nineteenth century produced the conditions for (at least embryonic) scholarship within schools beyond the classical confines of earlier ages. The ground was prepared, but we shall see that in the twentieth century that ground was at best neglected and at worst thoroughly despoiled.

What is common to any scholarly study is a sustained, strong, critical focus upon its subject matter, together with the desire to add to the fund of knowledge. Scholars display tenacity, intelligence and originality. They will take the trouble to be sure of their ground: it is imprudent to comment on a subject without detailed knowledge of that subject. Einstein is often misquoted (but with some justification, given his views) as having said that genius is ninety per cent perspiration and ten per cent inspiration. No doubt there have been discoveries requiring little sweat and toil; but scholars like Einstein usually have to work astonishingly hard for their achievements.

It seems that scholarship as such in our schools today is not highly prized – even though performance and results (and indeed the ubiquitous but deeply flawed league tables) are valued and perhaps over-valued. Even more alarming is the retreat from scholarship in schools, especially evident during the last forty to fifty years and if anything becoming more pronounced: this retreat is undermining the intellectual health of the nation. Whilst we may be foolish to expect the pupils to achieve the depth and breadth of Mill, we should endeavour to put them on the right path. We should expect those pupils who are likely to go on to the serious study of a subject at university to be given excellent foundations for this. There is much talk of 'good learning' in schools but too often the learning is routine, repetitive, and trivial. Teachers are now required to give much time to and expend much energy on tasks unrelated to their subjects: many confess that they have only rarely read a scholarly work since leaving university – with a few admitting that 'never' would be more accurate than 'rarely'. Professional development for teachers is too often focused upon those aspects of their teaching lives which are not related directly to their subjects. The leadership of schools is too often entirely preoccupied with non-curricular matters. Under government welfare reforms, schools must now liaise closely with doctors, social services, youth offending teams and the police. The retreat from the academic domain let alone from genuine scholarship is now a depressing fact of school life.

The character of scholarship is such that it may not appeal to or be right for all pupils – but it is very likely to attract those who are determined to gain places at the more competitive universities: academically selective independent schools have had great success in preparing their pupils for academically strong universities and so are well placed to promote scholarship. Central government appears to have a strong pragmatic and narrow utilitarian focus when it considers education: independent schools tend strongly to resist the worst consequences of this and are therefore predisposed to encourage a wider, richer educational diet. Hence, independent schools have a critical role to play in fostering scholarship. This is not to say that the state sector has no role but rather that it appears to be more difficult for state schools to foster scholarship when so many of them are required to balance the competing demands of vocational and of academic education; and very many teachers and leaders in the state sector willingly embrace a narrow utilitarian educational philosophy. For them to give unequivocal support to scholarship is most likely to be a daunting prospect. I distinguish such 'narrow' utilitarianism from the Utilitarianism of Mill: the latter being a well-defined philosophical position in which the rightness or wrongness of our moral and social actions is referred to the consequences of those actions.

An appreciation of the past and the changing perceptions of scholarship may help us see more clearly some of the issues involved. A scholar in England might once have gained recognition for the depth and thoroughness of his comprehension of the Classics – Thucydides, Plato, Cicero, Ovid, and other giants of antiquity. A classical education typically stayed within these limits, straying only perhaps to contemplate almost as a footnote some of the principle focal points of classical authorities – probably mathematics, philosophy, or astronomy. Of course, scholars then would also be required to give their close attention to the Bible (in Latin, Greek or perhaps Hebrew) – theology was always an eminently respectable field. However, the natural philosophers of the sixteenth and seventeenth centuries flattered their classical forebears (especially Aristotle) with considerable sincerity by imitating and indeed advancing their quest for knowledge of the natural world.

During the eighteenth and nineteenth centuries tensions arose, encouraged to a certain extent by intellectual and political change in France, between those who looked to a 'modern' age of reason and enlightenment and those who formed 'romantic' attachments to the cultural life of the past. Here, perhaps, we see the origins of the arts-science division exemplified in C.P Snow's *Two Cultures* which sees two groups: 'Literary intellectuals at one pole – at the other scientists …. [and] between the two a gulf of mutual incomprehension – sometimes hostility and dislike, but most of all lack of understanding.' Despite the battle lines which may have been drawn between rivals, by the middle of the nineteenth century language, morality, politics, geology, and even history – as well as the natural sciences – were fair game for the aspiring scholars. Indeed the twentieth century brought aesthetics (in its widest sense) and the mind itself clearly into the scholar's domain.

In the nineteenth century many urban grammar schools were under some pressure, frequently from local burghers, to modernize the curriculum: Mathematics, Science and Modern Languages came to be regarded as essential components of education. Narrow utilitarian attitudes began to prevail: subjects were frequently judged in terms of their usefulness to business and commerce. In 1859, Frederick Walker became High Master of The Manchester Grammar School – MGS – and immediately began to reform the school: his pupils were to be taught 'modern' subjects as well as the classics. Increasingly Head Masters did their best to ensure that through good teaching scholarship might flourish within grammar schools. Revolutionary scientific ideas and their industrial applications were taking centre stage, with the work of men of science like Faraday, Kelvin, and Maxwell. The ideas of Chemistry and Physics were gradually becoming part of the everyday life of pupils. Men such as Walker nevertheless regarded classical scholarship as the epitome of good learning: his best pupils studied little beyond Greek and Latin texts and only if they showed exceptional aptitude would they be allowed to spend time on Mathematics.

However, a key tension became evident in the nineteenth century: between the academic and scholarly aims of education and the pragmatic and vocational aims; and herein we may find an indication of the origins of the retreat from scholarship. One contemporary Mancunian, giving evidence to the Schools Enquiry Commission of

1865, reflected on the character of education at MGS thus: 'Being a free school, the grammar school is used by all classes of the community .... [but] the really poor are very scantily represented. Owing to its classical character, the grammar school is *par excellence* the school which clergymen, lawyers, and doctors affect for their children. The poor of Manchester do not think of using the school, because if they desire any education for their children, they desire only reading writing and arithmetic.' 'What is study for if not to prepare children for the workplace?' gives voice to a narrow utilitarian sentiment, still very evident today.

Despite their own classical inclinations, Walker and his contemporaries set the scene for an expansion of the curriculum which would allow the foundations of scholarship to develop in diverse subjects. Yet these foundations have been continually shaken in every part of the academic curriculum. The key difficulty here is the extent to which narrow utilitarian ambitions have subjugated academic subjects in the modern school curriculum, so that the point of studying German, Chemistry, or Geography is defined in terms of the usefulness of the subject to the economy, to the workplace, to the marketplace. Learning for learning's sake and the celebration of the intellect are not on this agenda.

Admittedly much learning does not automatically provide us with genuine scholarship. During the nineteenth century, there were many Mr Casaubons preoccupied with 'mouldy futilities' and many Pickwickian societies prepared to devote much energy to the search for mind-boggling revelations such as the source of the Hampstead Ponds. George Eliot and Charles Dickens both had a keen sense of the pointlessness and perhaps the absurdity of much supposed scholarly work at that time. An uncritical accumulation of information rarely if ever amounts to scholarship. Attending university was also no guarantee of a path to scholarship, even though for many this was where their education really began. Many students at Oxford and Cambridge were sent up to be gentlemen or sportsmen and became at best intellectual *dilettantes* rather than scholars.

The Education Act of 1870 brought about a transformation of education in our schools, encouraging and enabling (some 2500) local School Boards across the country to administer existing and build new schools. It was not until 1880 that there were sufficient places available for the Government to require that all children should be educated until the age of ten. Scholarship had little meaning for these poor 'scholars': elementary reading, writing and arithmetic dominated their studies – the limited aspirations of the poor noted above were being met. The sponsors of the Act aimed to produce a literate and numerate electorate: they were not concerned with bringing genuine scholarship to the wider populace.

John Stuart Mill was one of many who believed that without universal education and at the very least basic literacy for all, it would prove impossible for the electorate to judge what might best serve the common interest – or, in utilitarian terms, what might promote the greatest benefit and at the same time minimize any harm to society as a whole. Mill's vision of education was essentially liberal and individualistic: in *On Liberty* Mill argued that we should not allow 'that the whole or any large part of the education of the people should be in state hands' and that 'what the state should provide is financial support for children's education, in part or where necessary in whole .... and public examinations, extending to all children, and beginning at an early age'. He feared that, if education were to be left entirely in the hands of the state then this would be 'merely a contrivance for moulding people to be exactly like one another'. He did not object to the existence of a few state-maintained schools – but only if they provide beacons of excellence, setting the standard for independent schools! The irony of this is that, one hundred and fifty years later, many in government regard independent schools as establishing the standards for the state-maintained sector (not just academically but on the extra-curricular front and much else as well) – indeed, so much so that one government minister (Lord Adonis) has said that education in England needs the DNA of the independent sector.

Mill and those of a liberal disposition were not alone in warning against state control of education. In his *Critique of the Gotha Programme*, Karl Marx maintained that government and church alike should be excluded from any influence on schools. Here the danger is not the repression of individualism but rather the powerful (and Marx believed unwholesome) influence of the ruling class. In more recent times, the needs of those in power have been expressed by reference to the 'demands' of the economy; and in the second half of the twentieth century when 'we never had it so good', politicians of all persuasions have reminded us that education should prepare our children for the workplace as well as making them good citizens.

Liberal hopes for a genuinely independent educational system were dealt a serious blow by the Conservative government of 1902 when a new Education Act abolished school boards and transferred the command of schools to local 'educational' authorities with powers to establish new secondary schools as well as further to develop elementary schools. The Education Act of 1944 set the scene for two critical phases the consequences of which still preoccupy educationalists and politicians: the development of a tripartite (or more often than not bipartite) educational system; and the dismantling of that system to produce a single type of school – the comprehensive. It is likely that Mill would have seen this last development as perhaps the final nail in the coffin of his liberal dreams for education.

Rab Butler, Minister of Education and the architect of the 1944 Act, believed that the state should provide three different types of secondary school: grammar, technical and secondary modern – with each type of school providing a different kind of education for children of different abilities and aptitudes decided on the basis of examination. Importantly, many believed that the system would allow working class children to climb a ladder of opportunity, leaving their relative poverty behind. Few local authorities were able to establish technical schools – so in most cases only two types of school were available; and the eleven plus examination, which typically was used to determine which school a child should attend, was increasingly regarded as a 'pass-fail' test. Despite Butler's good intentions, there was no parity of esteem between the different types of school. Even so, many technical and some secondary modern schools produced extremely good results, relative to their intake; and not all grammar schools by any means got the best out of all their pupils.

Some local authorities assessed junior pupils not in a single 11+

examination but on the basis of many tests over time; and some authorities admitted late developers to grammar schools at ages 13, 14 or 16. However, possibly in the wider public mind – and certainly in the more prejudiced minds of the increasing number of sociologists and psychologists of education who tended to disregard counterexamples – Butler appeared to have created an unforgiving system, with the fate of pupils decided on a single day. Again, many regarded the ladder of opportunity as an opportunity for the middle classes to secure the future of their children and not as a foundation for social mobility.

The comprehensive system was devised to cure these educational ills, to produce greater equality and to improve social mobility. In 1965 a Circular from the Department for Education and Science instructed local authorities to replace the bipartite and tripartite structures with comprehensive schools. It would prevent children from being categorized at 11 and give them the freedom to develop their full potential. Working class children would have the same educational opportunities as others: indeed, where necessary, the Plowden Report of 1967 recommended that children in relatively deprived areas should be granted additional assistance. Whilst most local authorities complied with the 1965 edict, a few (e.g. Kent and Buckinghamshire) put up serious resistance and maintained 'state' grammar schools in their areas (and have continued to do so).

In 1976, the Prime Minister James Callaghan made a seminal speech at Ruskin College, Oxford – a speech which encapsulates what might be regarded as the latter-day 'received view' of the purpose and character of education. He said that: 'There is no virtue in producing socially well-adjusted members of society who are unemployed because they do not have the skills. Nor at the other extreme must they be technically efficient robots. Both of the basic purposes of education require the same essential tools. These are basic literacy, basic numeracy, the understanding of how to live and work together, respect for others, respect for the individual. This means acquiring certain foundational knowledge, skills and reasoning ability. It means developing lively inquiring minds and an appetite for further knowledge that will last a lifetime. It means mitigating as far as possible the disadvantages that may be suffered through poor home conditions or physical or mental handicap'. The specific language may have changed during the last thirty years (one no longer finds references to handicaps), but the message heard from those more recently in power differs in few essential details. One major change has been in the tone of the narrow utilitarian message: during the 1980s and 1990s, as central government took on more and more direct responsibility for education, schools and teachers (rather than government itself) were frequently criticized by those in power for 'failing the nation' – what some sociologists have called with some justice a 'discourse of derision'.

The year 1976 was important for many grammar schools which had held until then direct-grant status: they were maintained by a direct grant from the state together with means-tested funds for qualifying pupils from local authorities – supplemented by any endowment a school might possess. The move to the comprehensive system meant that most schools in this category had a stark choice: become independent without support from local authorities and central government or embrace the comprehensive ideal and relinquish their right to select on the basis of academic ability. Those schools without the resources or the nerve to break free from the state tended to abandon their semi-independent status. Others declared their intention to become fully independent, knowing that the impact upon social diversity would be significant: many families, previously supported by local authority scholarships, would not be able to afford the costs of an independent grammar school education. Few tears were shed in the town halls of urban (typically Labour-controlled) local authorities. However, plans emerged to deliver an alternative means of financing poorer children: the Assisted Places Scheme (brought in by Margaret Thatcher's Conservative Government in 1980) provided means-tested places for qualifying pupils at independent schools during the 1980s and 1990s. One of the first actions of the Labour Government of 1997 was to phase out the scheme. The main impact of this change was to make it all the more difficult for independent schools to maintain social diversity. A cynic might think that the last thing that any opponent of independent education might want would be independent grammar schools with a solid representation of pupils from poorer backgrounds. Such a cynic might subsequently have been confused by the political pressure brought to bear on the Charities Commission, through the Charities Act of 2006, to demand that independent schools should demonstrate public benefit by providing places for children of poor families.

In response to the end of the Assisted Places Scheme, a number of independent schools began to build means-tested bursary funds with some (like The Manchester Grammar School) amassing multi-million pound sums from appeals to ex-pupils and local interests with the aim of maintaining and where possible extending social diversity. Such schools did not need a Charities Act to tell them how to behave: widening social access was already part of their institutional DNA.

Independent schools have argued that they have two major advantages over state-maintained schools: they may select all of their pupils on the basis of academic (or other appropriate tests); and they are not required to follow any particular curriculum nor are they obliged to enter their pupils for any particular examinations. This second advantage acquired vital significance with the imposition upon the state-maintained sector of the National Curriculum together with associated national Key Stage assessments for children aged 7, 11 and 14: central government set down what should be taught, how it should be taught, and when pupils should be tested on what they have learnt. Despite the claims that teachers still had much room for manoeuvre, few really believed this. Indeed, with the increasing powers of the schools inspectorate to require that the teaching in and the management of state schools should follow prescribed patterns (or have very good reasons for not doing so), few have dared to 'step outside the box' – even if pupils and teachers are not being pressed into a single mould, the number of moulds available is now strictly limited. The situation is complicated by the fact that from time to time, central government has decided that one set of moulds is no longer 'fit for purpose' and has replaced it wholesale. What is not just acceptable but actually commendable one year is likely to be anathema the next: how children should be prepared in primary schools for the Key Stage examinations is a case in point here.

During the 1990s central government decided that central authority rather than the leadership of examination boards should shape public examinations at 16 (GCSE) and 18 (A-levels). At the same time, the vital influence of universities was diminished. As a consequence, the grip of central government (through its agencies the Qualifications and Curriculum Authority – QCA – and the Schools Inspectorate) on what was taught in schools and indeed on how it was taught became even stronger. This shift deserves serious attention.

Until the late 1990s, the content of a public examination was set down in a syllabus. Topics were set down often in a very general manner, allowing the examiners scope to range quite widely when setting questions. Different examination boards might offer quite different syllabuses for the same subject. Schools would be free to teach Physics (for example) relatively theoretically or with a greater emphasis upon experiment. Indeed, the same board might offer different approaches itself. For some, this meant choice and diversity – with teachers being able to select the approach which best suited local needs; others saw a not so glorious anarchy – with no guarantee that standards across and within boards, even for a single subject, were being maintained. Schools sometimes complained that what appeared in a question paper was too tenuously connected to an admittedly vague syllabus.

The arrival of modular examinations further complicated the plot. Pupils were free to take modules on more than one occasion, with the best mark counting. Some subjects lost their discrete identity: it was possible, for example, to gain an A-level in Chemistry with one-sixth of the work being done in Biology. Coursework too began to have a marked impact. One modular Science A-level allowed a third of the total marks to be awarded for coursework work done outside of the examination hall. For some, modules and coursework allowed pupils to engage enthusiastically and fruitfully with their subjects; others saw this as seriously undermining the gold standard in public examinations.

The response, planned by the Conservatives in the mid 1990s, but executed by the Labour Government in the late 1990s, was a dramatic review of the scope and character of A-level examinations. Curriculum 2000 was designed to revolutionize sixth form education: to establish a common, transparent framework for the examinations, to make A-level subjects accessible, to encourage more pupils to remain in education after the age of sixteen.

Some likened this change in importance to the amalgamation of O-levels and CSEs which provided a unified approach (the GCSE) in the 1980s. Others warned that the need to tackle the needs of the weaker students in our schools had become so dominant that the interests of the more able pupil were effectively being dismissed. Indeed, in some state schools regarding a child as very clever appears to be unacceptable: this is demonstrated by the failure of very many primary and a good number of secondary schools to embrace to any extent at all government schemes for gifted and talented pupils. Even though the majority of schools have co-operated, the impact has not been as helpful as desired – especially to those from poorer backgrounds.

The desire for transparency and accessibility brought about the introduction of 'specifications' and the demise of syllabuses. Whereas an A-level syllabus for a given subject tended to allow scope for examiners to probe around as well as within the content set down, a specification is much more prescriptive, specific and therefore (in examining terms) limiting in character: farewell to general and flexible references to items such as 'Momentum, elastic and inelastic collisions: formulae, applications and relevant experiments'; welcome to 'the student shall recall x, be aware that y, and understand z'. Setting straightforward examination questions becomes in some ways much easier. However, setting really challenging questions has become much more of a problem. Subjects have divided into digestible chunks and checklists have proliferated. Knowledge has been atomized, and the entire examination process has been infected with these 'microscopic' elements.

QCA, in response to concerns about providing adequate challenges for the more able sixth form students and with the approval of central government, introduced Advanced Extension Awards – intended to test the very best students. Few state schools took up this challenge and, because of this and other factors, few universities acknowledged AEA achievement. Now we look forward to a different strategy: the introduction of an A* grade, to be awarded to those gaining very high marks indeed at A-level. But high marks will not automatically signify the potential for genuine scholarship. This is why Oxford, for example, will continue to set its own examinations and tests for many subjects. When the best universities look for potential, they look (according to one Oxford admissions tutor) for students willing to find out more about subjects and to think about thinking, reading, writing and learning in new ways, for students able to develop sustained and independent thought. To what extent are we able to say that the present examination system is designed with such ends in mind?

Students now regard a detailed knowledge of how marking schemes are used by examiners as one of the most secure routes to examination success: they ask not 'What is the best answer?' but 'What response is expected here?' A-levels can and do pose tremendous challenges but the modern qualification race is more akin to low hurdles (and lots of them) rather than a steeplechase. Too much intelligence might actually be counter-productive: every academic school can provide examples of extremely able students who have been marked down simply because the examiner has not fully understood their argument. No examination system is perfect, but whilst the modern A-level is indeed more accessible and 'user-friendly', it has done scholarship no favours at all. Certainly there is little evidence of any requirement for the attributes of scholarship as defined earlier: 'a sustained, strong, critical focus upon its subject matter, together with the desire to add to the fund of knowledge'. Many schools have adopted the International Baccalaureate in part because this qualification offers more rigour and far greater challenges and definitely more scope for at least embryonic scholarship.

At GCSE, the challenges are understandably less exacting. However, many very able sixteen-year-old pupils fail to do themselves justice simply because they are bored almost to distraction. There is little doubt that O-level examinations were a far better preparation for more advanced work than GCSEs, which are characteristically pitched at the 'middle ground' to ensure that the vast majority of pupils are able to engage with the subjects under discussion. Many independent schools have adopted International GCSE qualifications to deal with this problem. For example, IGCSE Mathematics includes introductory but nevertheless challenging work using calculus, long absent from the home-based examinations at this level. The evidence shows that very many able pupils actually improve their performance considerably (by as much as a grade) when faced with these more serious challenges. The domination of coursework at this level has been most unfortunate: almost all such work is relatively trivial (for an able pupil) and requires a keen awareness of how the work will be marked as opposed to a deep understanding of the ideas involved; and any pupil daring to be original must do so with the utmost caution. Almost the reverse of scholarship is the order of the day.

Confused and confusing arguments about 'elitism' have not helped at all. Academically selective schools which promote scholarship are deprecated as elitist. Because the academic route has been given a preferred status in our society, because those in government have consistently presented a place at Oxbridge as the pinnacle of success, because the language of class division has been employed to deride those in the Middle Class with ambition for their children, we have reached an impasse.

The aversion to academic selection exacerbates the situation. Certain tasks in life require particular talents and those talents need to be nurtured. For example, ballet, football, or music: those wishing seriously to pursue any such career need specific education and training; and the earlier the work begins the better – it is rare to find someone flourishing without structured help. Equally, bringing dancers, footballers and musicians together, working with them together, considerably enhances the benefits to be gained: pupils learn from each other as well as from their teachers. For the very best, part-time preparation is insufficient: they must be wholly dedicated to the development of their talents. This need not make them narrow specialists – for that preparation can be ensure that wider perspectives are developed. Few appear to regard the strategies needed to produce first-class ballet dancers, footballers and musicians as problematic. However, if we replace the three examples chosen with another three, say mathematicians, linguists and engineers we run into difficulties. We can agree that not anyone will succeed as a concert pianist. We can agree that such talent can be identified relatively early and must be given special attention. We can agree that specialist music schools will greatly assist the pupil's progress. However, when the talents are academic, there is little agreement: at times the impression given is that with the right preparation anyone can be a first-class mathematician, linguist or engineer. A diluted academic education will serve the interests of a genuinely talented mathematician no more than a weekly ballet class will produce a Nureyev.

Those in government have found themselves between Scylla and Charybdis: on the one hand, they cannot give the impression that children of poorer families are typically suited only for vocational work; and on the other hand they need to respond to the genuine desire for appropriate training for the workplace from *inter alia* these same families and to the understandable demands of employers to produce an appropriately trained workforce. The 1944 Education Act was one attempt to overcome this predicament; the introduction of comprehensive schools another; and the successive attempts to promote accessibility at GCSE and Advanced levels yet others. The most recent strategy is based on a diploma programme for those aged 14-19, designed as a hybrid of the academic and the vocational: however, the academic content of such diplomas is unlikely to be any more exacting than the already diluted character of A-levels. However laudable such endeavours might be, there appears to be no determination to ensure a genuine parity of esteem between the vocational and the academic. If there were, then we would be able to recommend vocational as well as academic education to all children regardless of their background with enthusiasm and conviction. Instead of celebrating the vocational, we have diluted the academic and in so doing we may have made it almost impossible to reverse our collective retreat from scholarship.

Inspirational teaching is rarely done by those who remain on tramlines. The current examination system appears to have been devised to ensure that orderly, linear progress to a given terminus is paramount. There are no magical mystery tours here. Isaiah Berlin has some wise words for us in *The Power of Ideas*: 'Everyone knows what effect even the informal casual talk of a gifted, enthusiastic and sympathetic schoolmaster can have upon his pupils, for better and for worse'. Such talk can and does encourage capacities 'for discovery and invention, for basic research and original work' so that a pupil may feel very much 'at home in the intellectual world of his time'. If we are to attain (and perhaps exceed) Berlin's goal, at least for our most able pupils, then we must get off the tram and jump on a bus with a driver ready and willing to take frequent detours.

Alan Bennett's play *The History Boys* was inspired in part by the schoolboy experiences of the Royal National Theatre director Nick Hytner, who was a pupil at The Manchester Grammar School, a school where degrees of intellectual eccentricity and independence of mind and spirit amongst pupils and teachers have always been welcome. One typical reaction to the play, from journalist Benedict Nightingale, was this: 'I'd like to think that the play touches a contemporary nerve and confronts a contemporary anxiety. Isn't the nation of Shakespeare and Auden, Hardy and the great Gracie Fields descending into a slick philistinism? Isn't education becoming less a means of enriching minds than of greasing whatever mental wheels lead to success in the marketplace?' (As a Rochdalian I particularly appreciate Nightingale's inclusion of 'our Gracie' in his cultural catalogue.) Schools like MGS have tried to stand fast against the retreat from scholarship – and our ability to select (at ages 9, 10, 11, 12, 13, 14 and 16: not just at 11) on the basis of academic ability is a critical factor in this. However, the increasing control by central government of the educational world and the trivialisation of knowledge evident both in the educational domain and in the public conscientiousness make our task ever more difficult.

Although I believe that successive governments must shoulder much of the responsibility for the retreat from scholarship, there is a further important factor which must be considered, implicit in much that I have said so far: the growth of an educational relativism (or anti-realism) which can and often does trivialize our desire to comprehend the world, which refers knowledge to various cultural dispositions rather than to an objective 'real world', and which at its worst asserts that 'anything goes' in matters methodological as well as epistemological. The irony is that this growth has been encouraged by scholarship itself: many professional sociologists, psychologists and philosophers have mounted vigorous attacks upon the possibility of secure foundations for knowledge, against the realist's confidence that matters of fact may be decided by reference to the real world. If there is to be space for genuine scholarship in schools, then we must be ready to resist the seductive wiles of the relativists.

A realist outlook in philosophical terms should not be mistaken for the merely pragmatic or worldly wise. Although there are many varieties of realism (and indeed of relativist anti-realism), there is a shared confidence amongst realists that there is more to the world than our opinions of it. Metaphysically: there is something 'out there' independently of our minds – a real world, so to speak. Epistemologically: the truth or falsity of our knowledge is under-pinned by reference to the world. Methodologically: the methods we use to decide matters of fact are capable of delivering the epistemological goods.

The relativist message is subversive and essentially negative: it is not a programme, more a denial that any one programme makes sense, that any one account should have a preferred status. Whatever question faces us – about the causes of the Vietnam War, about the nature of electrons, about the symbolism in T.S. Eliot's *Journey of the Magi* – relativists will not allow the possibility of a definite answer, except within a particular world view, and they will remind us that other world views are no worse, and indeed no better, than the one in which we have chosen to operate. Right and wrong are relative to the view taken. Hence, right-for-me can be wrong-for-you without any contradiction or dilemma. Indeed, the very methods we may use to decide 'facts' depend upon our world view.

I have long found the relativist perspective troubling. First, a minor point: whilst the relativist might be correct to say that we can never be certain that we are right about anything one may ask the relativist why he is so sure that he must be right about the superiority of a relativist position – even the most extreme proponents of relativism recognize the delicious irony here. Secondly, and more important: I do not want to accept that apartheid, for example, is right for anyone or at any time – it is wrong, period. Hence, without the need for sophisticated arguments (which I could but will not rehearse here), I am opposed to relativism simply because the consequences of relativism are unacceptable.

In the hands of some, relativism can be a dangerous ideology. The unwary may come to believe that their opinion is just as good as any other. Yet in schools we are increasingly giving the impression that simply giving an opinion has a value in itself and is worth credit. Indeed, many pupils believe that their opinions are not just important but also well-founded – regardless of how precisely they are expressed and how cogently they are justified; and too many marking schemes reward this belief. Of course, many schemes will only give full marks for a given examination question to the pupil whose opinion is justified: I believe x for reasons y and z. At its best, there is nothing wrong with this. However, those who have scrutinized marking schemes (and most pupils have) will know that the hard-pressed examiner is looking for the stimulus of 'because' rather than the rightness of the answer. Rather like a rat in a psychology experiment:

press the 'right' button and a reward appears. At its worst, any response will do. What should merit reward is sound reasoning and not mere opinion.

Whilst we continue to see men and women in power who believe that political expedient and narrow utilitarian interests are more important that the life of the intellect, scholarship will be in danger. Is there hope? I believe very much that there is. Whilst independent schools are able to teach independently – without fear of too much government interference, we can continue to promote scholarship as much as possible. Whilst we are able to attract sufficient teachers with independent minds and spirits into the profession, teachers who are passionate about their subjects, we shall be able to take frequent detours from the linear routes determined by government, their agencies and examination boards. Whilst we are able to select on the basis of academic ability, we shall enable the most able pupils to fulfil their scholarly potentials. Whilst we remind our pupils of the need for sound reasoning and that the acquisition of knowledge is vital, fact and understanding will prevail over mere opinion. Whilst we are able to provide finance for those in need, we shall ensure that no able child, from whatever background, is denied an academic education and the foundations for genuine scholarship. However, without academic independent schools and without more independence for education as a whole – perhaps along the lines suggested by Mill in *On Liberty*, I fear that the retreat from scholarship in schools may prove to be irreversible.

THE HEAD SPEAKS

Author's Note

I am immensely grateful to Carol Ray and to colleagues Mark Coffey, Nick Munday, Paul Ponder, Andy Smith, and Justin Stanley, all of whom commented on earlier drafts.

THE MARY ERSKINE SCHOOL

(Formerly Edinburgh Ladies' College)

[Founded in 1694 by Mary Erskine and the Company of Merchants of the City of Edinburgh, the School was renamed in 1870 as the Edinburgh Educational Institution for Girls. It became the Edinburgh Ladies' College in 1889 and the Mary Erskine School in 1944. It is now one of the Erskine Stewart's Melville Schools, of which David Gray is the current Principal.]

'THE CHANGING FACE OF EDUCATION AND ITS ABIDING SPIRIT' (1937)

Mary Tweedie

Mary Tweedie writes in some detail about the changes in education in Scotland over seventy years – pointing out that there the education of girls has always been more closely connected with that of boys than in England and thus they are better provided for.

Miss Tweedie describes how the curriculum developed in Scotland: – the aim was to teach girls 'all that men are taught': Domestic training was stopped, except as 'cooking demonstrations'. She recalls an idyll of 'freedom', when the pace was slower and the pressure less:

Freedom of a kind existed, too, for the girls or 'young ladies' as they were called. They were permitted to walk in groups in the public gardens. They were easily granted exemption from classes and little pressure was brought to bear on the unwilling learner, while the home provided richly the hobbies, tramps and wide reading that are now interwoven with the school life. The pupil was even allowed a fallow time, if she was minded to take it, without undue questioning and without the modern injunction to 'bring a medical certificate'. The latter type of freedom worked well, it is true, in certain cases only, but it produced good things for the able and original mind.

But by 1937 education has been 'degraded in many places to mean the attainment at all costs of some ill-defined quantity of examinable knowledge into the school and university years'.

Miss Tweedie's thesis is that each new era has added to the school curriculum but taken nothing away. Specialists have all fought for the inclusion and expansion of their subjects. So girls are faced with an indigestible quantity of knowledge, and even if skilful timetabling can 'weave the mass into a coherent whole', still 'conflicting examination requirements take a heavy toll'.

Miss Tweedie believes that 'the motive spirit of a good school is freedom' and her summing up of girls' education in Scotland in 1937 is so full of enlightened good sense that it is reproduced fully:

The modern mind is franker and freer. Teachers and pupils were always potential friends. Today they easily become *comrades. Intercourse is less hampered by discipline. Fear and nervousness are watched for and combated by laughter and kindness. Physical difficulties are sympathized with and latent abilities are encouraged. Discipline is free. The small child can say to her Head Mistress: 'Oh no, I am not afraid of <u>you</u>,' and the older one can – and does – argue freely. They bring their difficulties – we do not call then complaints – and so there has grown up a joint belief that the misrepresentations of immature minds are not untruths, that a fallow time is often a physical or psychological phase, that nervousness is not a disease requiring drugs, that right food is an essential part of education, that latent capacity is brought out by encouragement better than by strict measures, that a practical course is as honourable as an academic one, that less homework can often give better results, that age is not necessarily chronological, that individuals develop at different rates, that school regulations are for the mutual good and that confidence between home and school is an essential ingredient of good work.*

THE CHANGING FACE OF MARY ERSKINE

David Gray

Born in 1629, and living to the grand old age of seventy-nine, Mary Erskine lived, not only to see her girls' school founded in 1694, and successfully established in the years following, but also to see it acknowledged and ratified by the penultimate act of the old Scottish Parliament immediately before the Act of Union took effect in 1707.

The school, (then known as the Merchant Maiden Hospital), owing to Mary Erskine's shrewd negotiations with Edinburgh's foremost livery company, the leading protagonist in the development of Edinburgh's commercial influence in the seventeenth century, was the first to provide education exclusively for girls in the United Kingdom and was loosely modelled on the schools of Louis XIV in France.

Mary Erskine had had a tough life. Twice widowed, she bore, by her first husband, Robert Kennedy, her only child, a daughter, Euphemia, who died at the age of five. She worked as a chemist on the High Street in Edinburgh, opposite St Giles' Cathedral, but had become wealthy through the acquisition of property from her second husband, James Hair. As a money lender in the years before the Bank of Scotland was founded in 1695, she was the people's banker. On the interest earned, at the age of 65, she was able to turn to Edinburgh's merchants with a sizeable sum and propose that by their matching her offer, their daughters might benefit from the education already provided elsewhere for their sons. As an insurance policy against their untimely deaths, in what was in those days adventurous but risky work, the merchants found Mistress Erskine's offer irresistible.

Mary Erskine's philanthropy, perhaps the result of being without heirs, or in memory of her only daughter, or through the scars of battling against the odds in a man's world, would not have been out of place, and almost certainly would have been more readily acknowledged, in the nineteenth century, when fortunes made at the height of the British Empire, offered opportunity for largesse at home, in an age of growing Victorian reform. Her commercial drive and competitive edge would not have been out of place in the twentieth century when Mary Erskine might well have been a household name, like Laura Ashley or Anita Roddick, figures of our own age, as a beacon to which the modern woman might aspire.

All the more remarkable then that Mary Erskine's vision, to provide 'at book, bed and board' education for the daughters of burgesses of the City of Edinburgh, was spawned two centuries earlier in Scotland, where, in spite of John Knox's school in every parish, education for the 'fairer sex' was hardly fashionable.

That early education aimed to inculcate in girls reading, writing and rudimentary mathematics, enabling them to master domestic accounts and household management. Government gurus today dress up similar fundamental concepts in terms of literacy, numeracy, health, nutrition and citizenship, but could teach little, that had not been already learned, to the first girls at the Merchant Maiden Hospital, who might have reciprocated with lessons on thrift and on the exercise of good sense, for the benefit of contemporary education chiefs.

By late Victorian times, the school had moved to Queen Street at the heart of Edinburgh's New Town, established in the prosperity of the Georgian era. The move was significant in that it followed the great Education Reform Act making compulsory the provision of education for children up to the age of twelve. The governors of the school therefore determined to change its nature from that of a 'hospital' providing board to that of a day school in the modern sense. When the school opened in new premises on Queen Street in 1871, it boasted over 600 girls. The curriculum provided for girls had changed too, with emphasis on the study of modern languages, French and German, and on the sciences, as well as elements of a more classical education. These changes owed less to the changing status of women over 200 years than to the growth and expansion of the British Empire and to the consequences of the Industrial Revolution and its associated technologies. This had triggered more effective nationwide communication and forms of transport which facilitated, at least for the middle classes, comfortable, swift and safe travel to far off places.

The Mary Erskine School product of the late nineteenth century may have been an independent thinker, a cosmopolite of sorts, even a university graduate. But, settling into middle age, while she may have successfully aspired to the doughty deeds of her school's founder, it is more likely that she would have become the matriarchal figure synonymous with Victorian Britain.

The First World War and the subsequent widespread employment of women of all classes in industrial Britain in responsible as well as menial positions, the introduction of universal suffrage, the decline of Empire and an incipient meritocracy altered expectations in the first half of the twentieth century for girls attending The Mary Erskine School. By 1937, The Mary Erskine parents required their daughters to emerge from their schooling with qualifications which would fit them either for Higher Education or for further training or for employment. They saw too the benefits of what would now be termed as extra curricular activity, although they perceived their advantages to be of a practical nature rather than associate them with some kind of more abstract personal development. So it was that participation in team sports or individual athletic exercise was good for the health, while playing the piano was a useful accomplishment for demonstration later to potential suitors or to entertain the children. Although the academic education provided to the girls was not radically different from that of the late nineteenth century, it was applied with greater intensity and rigour and to a more specific, utilitarian end.

By 1950, many Mary Erskine girls went on to university in an era where that remained largely the preserve of the male. Some went into elevated positions in the Civil Service, others to the professions and a few into academic research, but there was an apartheid involuntarily practised by which those who were perceived as being capable of being 'blue stockings' became so. Those who were not, but yet who were highly capable, were regarded too often as second class citizens; they went on to form the backbone of the country as nurses, caterers, clerks, secretaries. Some of those former pupils of the mid twentieth century, aware of their capacities and of the changing role of women in British society, retain resentment to this day of their unwitting compartmentalization by the School on the basis of perceived academic ability. Most, however, in the spirit of resilience of the School's founder, went on to lead defiantly successful lives.

The Governors of the school recognized that by the 1960s the elegant, but cramped, environment of the school for 600 girls, in which the playground was a roof garden and the playing fields were sited at a distance of two miles, was inappropriate. Having purchased 100 acres of suburban land with a Georgian house at its centre, they determined to build a modern school. As the move to Queen Street had been significant, so was this one in that the construction of new buildings, surrounded by beautiful rolling grounds, provided an occasion to create a new philosophy of education for Mary Erskine girls.

The buildings were spacious, light and included public spaces for theatrical and musical performance, library study, assemblies, more intimate meetings and communal dining. A swimming pool, and capacious playing fields surrounding the academic departments and including all weather surfaces for tennis and hockey and attractively landscaped avenues of trees in which to stroll, completed the picture. The academic departments were capaciously housed and none was neglected, from Physics to Home Economics and from History to Mathematics. The physical design was symptomatic of the holistic education which the Governors of the school recognized was required for the education of girls in the modern world, in which each individual would compete on equal terms and in which versatility, good communication skills and talents of every kind would be required for Britain's post Empire, pluralistic society.

And so, while new buildings and departments have since appeared, (a Prep Department for three to five year olds, a burgeoning ICT Department, and the addition of subjects such as Spanish and Computing), reflecting changes in technology and life styles, new trends in the world's economies and the emergence of the concept of the global village, the philosophy has remained constant.

In post 2000 Britain, education needs to be dynamic and flexible to suit the changing world in which we live. For girls, their diverse talents need to be identified, nurtured and promoted by whatever means so that their levels of self-esteem, confidence and self-knowledge are such as to face a demanding world with equanimity. The modern Mary Erskine girl enters careers as varied as medicine, fashion design, astrophysics, surveying, banking, engineering, marketing, media production and law. But the stimulation of intellectual curiosity, the filling of the precious vessel with knowledge and the delivery of academic qualifications are far from being adequate to prepare her for a world in which at least 40% of young people in the United Kingdom become undergraduates and in which Britain competes, often on unfavourable terms, with the ambitious economies and the work hungry populations of Eastern Europe, the Asian sub continent and the Far East.

Every moment the Mary Erskine girl is at school matters, for school is her microcosm of society, its rules reflecting the wider nation's laws. She needs to learn to abide by them but equally, through representation on the School Council, or through debating, or the School's societies, or the Youth Parliament, or the School newspaper, she must learn to understand their premises, work constructively through their infrastructure, question their failings and promote improvement. She needs to have a voice and learn to use this at school in such a way as to develop both awareness of the world around and beyond her and the confidence to be heard and listened to long after school has been left behind. The extra curricular programme, whether through sporting activities, musical or dramatic participation, through the Combined Cadet Force or the Duke of Edinburgh's Award, is designed to draw out undiscovered inclinations, gifts or strengths, while also teaching the rudiments of success and good citizenship in a modern democracy: individual skills are important, winning and performing to the very highest standards possible matter, and all of these will only lead to achievement and happiness if team work is practised effectively.

But perhaps the greatest difference in The Mary Erskine School of 1937 to that of 2007 has been the iconoclastic change from single sex education as a dogma to single sex education as a practical means to an end. The Erskine Stewart's Melville Schools today combine the best of both worlds: co-education in the years prior to adolescence, and also for the final year of senior school as a transition to Higher Education and employment, by which time, boys and girls, their confidence at its height, can happily compete and collaborate together, in the laboratory, in the classroom, in the workshop and, in roles of responsibility, and can begin the task of management, which, after school, will dominate their lives.

But in that uncertain period in between childhood and adulthood, that shadowy, no man's land in which every footstep is fraught with doubt and in which identities are easily suppressed in self-consciousness or disguised by atavistic tendencies, that period otherwise known as adolescence, girls and boys are still best served by being taught separately, allowing their natural intelligence and their individual insights to flourish without the distraction, dominance or bullying tendencies of the other sex. So it is that without the speculative qualities of boys, girls will speculate to fill the vacuum, while boys, without the conscientiousness of girls with which to compete, will happily compete amongst themselves, the danger of humiliation by 'the fairer sex' at an age at which their egos are most vulnerable, removed.

At The Mary Erskine School then, quite apart from the linguists, artists, musicians and literary types, whom you might anyway expect to find, mathematicians, scientists, architects and engineers also flourish in numbers. Thus prepared in that which they are, by nature, rather than by convention, talented, they are more likely to compete effectively in an unforgiving, highly competitive world. And under such conditions, they are more likely to be happy.

But single sex education should not be an inflexible doctrine which is why, outside adolescence, it is not practised at the Erskine Stewart's Melville Schools and why within adolescence it is tempered throughout that period by boys and girls from both schools working together to foster social development in collaborative ventures, such as musicals, concerts, outdoor education, and through inter House competitions, where mixed teams pit their wits and skills throughout the school year in everything from General Knowledge to Basketball.

THE HEAD SPEAKS

Mary Erskine was a woman before her time. Self aware, confident, resilient, ambitious, socially responsible, she embodied all the qualities required for success in any age. Her education was 'the slings and arrows of outrageous fortune' hurled at her throughout her life. Her vision was to create an environment in which girls, forewarned, could be forearmed. Successive generations of Governors, Principals, Heads and teachers have tailored her school to the cloth of the age, while bearing in mind, in guiding girls across the centuries, her personal example, and the school's motto, which embodies her spirit: 'mitis et fortis' – gentle and strong.

MILL HILL SCHOOL

'EDUCATION FOR TOMORROW' (1936)

M. L. Jacks

In a remarkably perceptive essay, M. L. Jacks suggests that schools have to worry not about the world as it is now, but as it will be in future: 'We have to educate not for a changed world, but for a world that is changing all the time'. He points out that the era has gone when 'certain fundamental axioms of good and evil, right and wrong, were accepted without question'. As a result, 'many parents have abdicated, and look to the school more and more for the control and organization of their boy's life'. So as well as teaching school subjects, teachers have to educate their pupils in good manners, direct their interests and friendships, organize their holidays, and find jobs for them when they leave. Seventy years on, with the pace of change if anything faster, most Head Teachers would share Jacks's observation of the responsibilities now thrust on schools.

First, Jacks sees God as the necessary centre of school life – all the more important when the world is in flux and throughout Europe, in the absence of any moral standpoint, the young are being drawn to authoritarian movements – Fascism, Nazism, Communism. Interestingly Jacks also lists Roman Catholicism, Fundamentalism and the Group Movement among the dictatorships which are inadequate for human needs.

Secondly, Jacks sees Public Schools as potentially in 'ignorance of what is going on outside its walls and of the people who live there' (a subject to which Dominic Luckett returns below). While acknowledging the efforts of schools to engage with poorer communities and, for example, to visit depressed areas and participate in joint 'working camps' with the unemployed, Jacks argues the need for the study of international affairs and for junior international summer schools where boys of different nationalities 'live, work, and play together'. With Europe teetering on the brink of war, Jacks believes that the common sense of the young 'may yet save the world for peace, but a new significance must be given to old conceptions of citizenship, of power, patriotism, and public service':

> *Power is seen to be the power to help, and not to hurt, the power to give, and not to grab. Patriotism is the devotion to a country which has some noble contribution to make, which it and it alone can make, to the welfare of humanity, and not to one which desires to paint more and more of humanity's world red.*

Thirdly, Jacks sees the need for intellectual discipline. Boys must be taught to think:

> *This is one of the prime justifications for the traditional school subjects, which some decry and would oust from the*

curriculum in favour of more supposedly 'useful' subjects. They must never be ousted.

Only if they think can the insidious power of the press and the 'wireless' be combated. There is value, too, in being made to do things that don't appeal to us:

> *The fact of the matter is that life imposes on each one of us many uncongenial tasks, and that any preparation for life must bear that in mind and act accordingly. Here is an answer to those modernists in educational theory who say that the teacher's business is to find out what a child likes doing and is good at, and let him concentrate on that: it is the doctrine of self-expression, but self-mastery comes first, and unless that is learnt the resulting self won't be worth expressing.*

Finally Jacks argues for the co-education of mind and body: there is a need 'to raise the whole status of physical training, and to apply to the body all those educational principles which we have long applied to the training of the mind'.

EDUCATION FOR TOMORROW

Dominic Luckett

Much has changed since Maurice Jacks contributed to the original edition of *The Head Master Speaks*. To Jacks, such change would have come as no surprise, for it is one of the central themes of his piece that schools, and those who work within them, need to prepare young people not for the world as it is, but for the world as it is likely to be in the future. As he quite rightly said, 'We have to educate … not for a changed world, but for a world that is changing all the time'.

Since Jacks's departure from the School, Mill Hill has, like a great many such institutions, undergone significant structural changes. The relatively small, predominantly boarding, boys' only school of his era has become a much larger, co-educational establishment in which day pupils significantly outnumber their boarding counterparts. Attitudes, too, have moved on since Jacks's time. Although, for example, few would now disagree with his condemnation of the Nazi and Fascist regimes then in the ascendant in Europe, his jibe against the Roman Catholic 'dictatorship' strikes a rather discordant note. (Jacks would, no doubt, have been disturbed to discover that Mill Hill began its third century in 2007 with a new, Catholic Head Master .…)

But while some of Jacks's views, reflecting those of society more generally, may strike us as odd, what is far more arresting is the extent to which the underlying dynamics of his very different world are similar to those of our own. Jacks laments the decline in the moral certainties that characterized his own boyhood, when 'certain fundamental axioms of good and evil, of right and wrong, were accepted without question'. He notes the decline of traditional family life, the growth in secularism, the youthful obsession with novelty and the ever-increasing pace of change, all of which he believed were making life less predictable and, by implication, more dangerous. He also draws attention to the importance of the 'wireless waves', foreshadowing the impact that the internet would have upon the young and, aside from its many benefits, the new problems that it would bring, from cyber-bullying to the use of chat rooms by predatory paedophiles.

While Jacks was concerned about the well-being of society at large, he was acutely aware of the need to think about the place that schools such as his occupied within that society; and for anyone leading an independent school at the start of the twenty-first century few issues are more important. At the same time as the independent sector has reached new heights of popularity with parents, it has also been called upon to justify its existence in a way that requires a thorough, honest and open-minded self-assessment of its role and its contribution. So, what part do the independent schools have to play in modern Britain, and how can they play that part more effectively in the decades to come?

One of the most obvious ways in which independent schools contribute to society is by setting a benchmark of excellence in education. To take a crude measure, pupils from independent schools do, on average, better at A level than those from maintained schools.

Currently just over 25% of all A levels are awarded A grades. In independent schools, the figure is almost double, at around 48%. Part of this discrepancy is, of course, accounted for by the differing ability profile of those entering the two sectors. But while many independent schools are academically highly selective, many are not. Indeed, for large numbers of independent schools, their very survival depends upon taking pupils of modest academic ability. So the fact that almost half of all A level examinations taken by boys and girls in independent schools result in A grades does say a great deal about the quality of teaching and learning across the independent sector.

Inevitably, given their success at A level, independent school pupils tend to do well in competition for places at the leading universities. Most notably, and despite increasing claims of bias against privately educated applicants, Oxford and Cambridge still award almost half their places to pupils from such schools. Whatever our detractors may say, this is for no other reason than that independent schools educate their young people well, maximizing their potential and thus giving their brightest pupils the opportunity to compete successfully, and in large numbers, for places at the most sought after universities. Indeed, it must be something of a headache for university admissions tutors when, faced with quotas designed to limit the number of independent school applicants they admit, they find many of their strongest applicants coming from just such schools.

Of course, the success of independent school pupils at A level also says something about the value of A levels as a discriminator between the bright, the very bright and the simply well-taught. But in this respect, too, independent schools have made a major contribution, pioneering the introduction of new academic qualifications which give universities and employers more precise means of distinguishing between the most able. Most obviously, it has been largely through the initiative of independent schools that the International Baccalaureate (IB) has penetrated into this country. There are currently just over one hundred institutions in the UK teaching towards the IB diploma. The great majority are independent schools. Such has been their success that, in November 2006, Prime Minister Blair announced that the Department for Education and Skills (now the Department for Children, Families and Schools) would be seeking to ensure that at least one institution in every local authority outside London would be offering the IB. That independent schools have been able to blaze this trail is precisely because of their independence. Relatively free from the influence of party political agendas, it is possible for the educational practice of each school to be determined by its own educationalists, rather than dictated by politicians. And that can only be a good thing.

The very academic success of independent schools does, however, carry with it the danger that this is the element of their work on which they may tend to focus, to the detriment of other important things. One reason for this is the supposed measurability of academic achievement through examination league tables. It can certainly be comforting, for Heads, governors and parents alike, to be presented with a simple, rank-order of schools. Such ranking appears to make the choice of school easier for parents, and appears to offer schools an opportunity to demonstrate objectively how effectively they are going about their business. Sadly, life is not nearly so simple. First, any attempt to use league table positions to compare the performance of schools is fatally undermined by the fact that the various tables are put together in differing ways. While this may allow schools to pick and choose which table to use in their marketing, depending upon which gives them the most favourable position, it does nothing to add credibility to the league tables themselves. Secondly, even if there were not this problem of variability between tables, they are still, for very obvious reasons, deeply misleading devices. They take, for example, no account of 'value added' (the amount of progress a pupil makes in the years leading to his or her examinations). They thus fail to distinguish between a school that does well in the tables simply because it has an intake of exceptionally bright children, and one that enjoys a similar position because it helps pupils of modest ability to make more progress during their GCSE, A level or IB courses.

It has become routine for Heads and others to denounce examination league tables as ill-conceived, misleading and confusing. Yet too many, behind this façade of condemnation, still play the league table game, seeking to use their school's current position to validate their claims about their success in educating their pupils. The problem with this is that while league tables do say something, albeit imperfectly, about relative performance in public examinations, they ignore everything else that goes on in a school. It is this exclusive focus upon one aspect of the educational enterprise that makes the tables so dangerous, seducing some schools into throwing all their eggs into this one educational basket and placing undue emphasis on the need for examination success.

The schools which have succumbed to this temptation have set out their stall clearly and unambiguously as providers of a narrowly academic education. This may serve the interests of a Head intent on rapid advancement, but it is hard to see how such an approach can benefit any individual child. True, it may help him or her to gain slightly higher grades (although whether it actually does is highly debatable – a point to which I shall return), but even small improvements can come at a huge cost. By concentrating too much on academic endeavours, schools deny their pupils the opportunity to spend more time playing sport, expanding their cultural horizons through trips to the theatre, concerts, and galleries, and (most importantly) exploring their own interests. Above all, they rob their pupils of the space to develop as human beings, to play, and to develop the rounded personalities that will help them lead successful and happy lives. And let us not forget that spectacular examination results almost never, on their own, lead to successful careers. Good sixth form qualifications and a respectable degree are of undoubted importance in allowing young people to clear the first hurdle of securing a job interview. Thereafter, it is how they come across when interviewed, the warmth of their personality, their awareness of the outside world, and their ability to enter the workplace as balanced, functioning human beings, that counts most. If we provide pupils with an overly-narrow education, we rob them of the chance to grow in ways that will set them on the path to success in their chosen field.

Even more fundamentally flawed is the belief that an education based only on academic lines will necessarily lead to examination achievement. There is, in fact, no conflict between genuine scholarship and the provision of a broad, balanced education. Those schools which believe that academic success can only be gained by focusing solely upon examination results simply misunderstand the way in which academic and extra-curricular successes feed off each other. To succeed in one area only serves to give young people the confidence they need to flourish in all their endeavours. As educators, we should be primarily interested in helping our young people feel secure, cared for, fulfilled and happy. For when we do that, they will be much more likely to do well in the academic side of life and in their other pursuits. It was this genuinely holistic and balanced educational experience in which Maurice Jacks (who moved on from Mill Hill to become Director of Oxford University's Institute of Education) believed. Anything else is to treat the various facets of our children's lives and personalities as discrete entities, and to ignore the inter-connectedness that makes them what they are.

An excessive focus on the academic also runs the risk of divorcing our independent schools from their heritage and from what has made them such a vital contributor to so many aspects of our national life. It is true that the independent schools have provided this country with far more than their fair share of outstanding academics, including the Nobel Laureate geneticist Francis Crick, an Old Millhillian from the time of Maurice Jacks. Yet, aside from the academic life of the country, the products of independent schools have always made enormous contributions to the nation's sporting, cultural, artistic, political and commercial life. For them to continue to do so, they must avoid becoming places of narrow, exam-driven preoccupation.

One of the great challenges, then, for an independent sector seeking to serve the needs of the country in the twenty-first century is to continue doing what it has always done: to serve as beacons of excellence in all areas, helping children to fulfil their potential by offering a wide, balanced and forward-looking curriculum. Of course, that does not mean that they can stand still. As Jacks emphasized, success in education demands that schools cater for more than just the needs of the present. They must look to the future, and prepare the young for the world that is not yet here. A further challenge, however, is for independent schools to spread their unquestionable benefits to a wider public, and to bring into their orbit children from families for whom the cost of private education is simply prohibitive.

For many years, independent schools have played a significant, but often unrecognized, part in promoting social cohesion through their ability to bring together boys and girls from different cultural, ethnic, linguistic and religious traditions. This has particularly been so at boarding schools, whose houses and dormitories have served as meeting places for children from across the world. At present-day Mill Hill, for example, no fewer than thirty-six nationalities are represented among the pupils. Such cosmopolitanism has lent many schools a rich, diverse and vibrant texture and has allowed their pupils to move out into the world with a greater understanding and feel for other cultures and traditions than many who have not enjoyed this advantage. In a world so fractured by mistrust and suspicion, this has seldom been more important. Where our schools have not been so successful has been in taking pupils from a comparably broad social spectrum.

One measure of the success of modern independent schools is the number of parents now choosing to pay for their children's schooling. Independent schools currently educate over half a million children, representing roughly 7% of the school children in this country and some 23% of those in the sixth form (thus saving the taxpayer over £2 billion each year). Given these numbers, it should be obvious that independent schools are not the elitist and anachronistic nurseries for the wealthy and privileged that many still imagine them to be. Indeed, many of the parents who choose to place their sons and daughters in the independent sector are only able to do so because they are prepared to make considerable personal sacrifices, foregoing holidays, new cars and other personal gratifications in order to provide their children with the best educational opportunities available.

However, it remains the case that independent schools are extremely expensive. That is not their fault. The costs of running a school are high, not least because of the substantial wage bill that each has to pay. But the fact remains that for most families in this country independent education remains an unaffordable luxury. In 2006-07, according to figures produced by the Independent Schools' Council, the average termly fee was £3,391, whilst the average termly boarding fee was significantly higher, at £6,712. Thus, even a day place is likely to cost upwards of £9,000 per child, per year of post-tax income, something that is well beyond the reach of most families (the majority of which have more than one child).

It is true that just over 30% of pupils enjoy some form of financial support from their school, mostly in the form of scholarships and bursaries. However, with fees as they are, even a substantial reduction in fees still excludes the majority of families from considering the option of private education. It is this fact that provides the independent sector with its greatest challenge: how to broaden access and spread the benefits of private education, thus allowing our schools to be vehicles for the promotion of social cohesion, rather than perpetuators of social and economic division.

There is, of course, nothing new about independent schools seeking to make themselves accessible to those from families of modest means. There is a very well established tradition of places at independent schools being offered to such boys and girls. Many such places have been funded from individual schools' own resources. Some have been able to rely upon endowments, most obviously at Christ's Hospital in Sussex. Founded in 1552 by Edward VI to care for poor children from the capital, the school derives only around 16% of its income from parental contributions. Sadly, most independent schools have nothing like the resources needed to fund such a level of support. Many, like Mill Hill, have very modest endowments on which to draw for bursaries, and instead take a portion of their fee income to provide bursary support. In this way, parents at most independent schools not only save the Exchequer money that would otherwise have to be spent on a maintained school place, but also help to subsidize many of those who receive bursaries.

The benefits of broadening access to independent schools were nowhere more appreciated than at Mill Hill in the years during and immediately following Maurice Jacks's Headmastership. It was Jacks's contention that one of the great challenges for his generation was to 'widen the field on which the Public Schools draw'. This was vital, he believed, for the good of the schools themselves, in order to combat the ever-present danger of 'extraordinary ignorance of what is going on outside its walls and of the people who live there'. At the same time, there were those outside the independent schools who also believed in the benefits to be derived through the broadening of access. In a development first seriously mooted as early as 1939, and formally coming into existence through the provisions of the 1944 Education Act, pupils from families of modest means were able to enter the school under the Middlesex Scheme, their fees being paid by Middlesex County Council.

Although other schools also participated, it was at Mill Hill that the venture was perhaps most successful, with up to one fifth of the school being funded under the Scheme's provisions. Through the Scheme, the school gained an element of diversity and inclusivity that enriched and enlivened it. The Middlesex Scheme came to an end with the abolition of the Middlesex County Council, but until the late 1990s, the Assisted Places Scheme offered, at Mill Hill and other schools, similar opportunities for access. With the ending of Assisted Places, it has been left to schools themselves to find ways of ensuring that their doors remain as widely open as possible.

It is, of course, the case that the 2006 Charities Act has focused attention on the issue of access. As a result of the Act, independent schools will no longer be considered to merit charitable status just because they provide an educational service. Rather, those (the majority) that enjoy such status need to demonstrate a clear 'public benefit'. Exactly how they are expected to do this remains unclear. However, it is believed by many that the best way will be for schools to extend their bursary provision and thus widen access to the educational benefits that they offer.

This may be true, and the Charity Commissioners may indeed be impressed by institutions which extend the number of pupils they admit from modest or poor backgrounds. But this rather misses the point. The drive to open up access to independent schools should not be undertaken simply as a means to satisfy a politically-inspired test administered by the Charity Commissioners. It should be done because it is inherently a good thing to do. And, as Jacks noted, it is not merely something that is beneficial for those boys and girls who stand in receipt of free or heavily-subsidized places (though the range of opportunity – academic, sporting, artistic, extra-curricular – open to independent school pupils is usually far greater than that available to their maintained school contemporaries). It is also of profound benefit for every independent school to have a pupil populace made up of children from a wide variety of backgrounds, ensuring that they remain socially aware and diverse institutions. It is a situation in which everybody wins.

The ability of schools to offer bursaries depends, at least in part, upon how wealthy they are. The richer the school, the easier it is for it to divert money into bursary funds, to appeal to wealthy parents and alumni, or to seek assistance from the livery companies or other charitable foundations to which they might be connected. It is the smaller, poorer schools with less illustrious and less numerous old boys and girls who are likely to find it more difficult to locate the money that can be used to offer free or heavily-subsidized places. And it is important not to forget the potential impact upon fee-paying parents of the drive to secure funds for bursaries. Already, at most independent schools, every UK tax-paying parent pays three times for their child's education. First, they pay the independent school fees.

Secondly, they pay part of their tax bill to fund the state school place which their children are not taking up. Thirdly, part of the school fees they pay are allocated automatically to the school's bursary fund. As a result, schools have to exercise a certain caution in asking parents to contribute a fourth time, through fundraising appeals designed to secure additional bursary funds for children from less affluent backgrounds. Some wealthy parents can certainly afford to help in this way, but for others it is simply asking too much.

Yet the problem of widening access lies only partly in finding the money to fund bursary places. An equally significant problem lies in identifying and attracting pupils who might benefit from independent education. *The Times* recently carried an advertisement placed on behalf of nineteen of London's independent schools alerting readers to the fact that they were each offering free or subsidized places. While this is commendable, it does raise questions as to the sort of families these schools are hoping will apply for their bursary-funded places – those from genuinely disadvantaged families, the sort whose sons and daughters would most benefit from the chances offered by private education, tend not to read *The Times*. Either the marketing managers responsible for this advertisement have failed to appreciate that simple fact, or the schools were never intending to recruit from outside the middle classes.

If independent schools are to use what bursaries they can offer to real effect, they need to work hard to access boys and girls from families for whom private education has never been seen as an option. The efforts of Oxford and Cambridge Universities to reach out to such families have been going on for some time, and they have found it extremely hard to gain a foothold in communities beyond their traditional middle class catchment. But the difficulty of the task should not deter schools from trying, for it is by broadening our social make-up that we will be best able create the socially diverse communities of learning that will be the hallmark of the successful independent schools of the twenty-first century.

An example of how independent schools can work together with charitable organizations to give a chance to young people from disadvantaged backgrounds comes from Rugby School's work with the Eastside Young Leaders Academy. The Academy works with young African and Caribbean boys at risk of social exclusion and aims to give them the structure, discipline and opportunities that will lead them away from crime and enable them to become leaders of tomorrow. In September 2007, two of the Academy's boys took up places as boarders at Rugby as a result of the award of bursaries funded by the School's Arnold Foundation. And if other schools wish to make a genuine difference, it should be through associations such as this, rather than advertisements in *The Times*, that they should be seeking to work.

There are other ways, too, in which independent schools should be seeking to extend their reach. An obvious route is through involvement with the government's Academies programme, where the government is actively seeking to promote close co-operation between successful independent schools and Academies. Although involvement is not yet as advanced as it could and should be, there are encouraging signs that it is taking root, with some twenty schools already involved as sponsors or in other ways. Such co-operation is something which Maurice Jacks believed could be of huge benefit. He declared that 'there is a great future for [independent] schools in association with the national system'.

Sadly there are limits to what the independent sector can do. The combined number of independent schools is far smaller than the total in the maintained sector. The resources at their disposal vary widely, but most struggle to make a modest surplus, even in the prosperous times that the country has enjoyed for the past decade. So the notion that the independent sector is sufficiently wealthy to allow it to subsidize the ailing state sector to a significantly greater degree than it already does is deeply misguided. Yet the fact remains that independent schools of all sorts and sizes collectively provide a model for how excellence in education can be achieved.

That said, the independent sector is certainly not perfect, and it is far from true that all the best schools in the country are independent: there are many, many maintained schools from which the independent sector could learn a great deal about (for example) the promotion and achievement of excellence through good practice in teaching and management. And here perhaps is the key: it is through partnership, in the broadest sense, between independent and maintained schools that Britain will once more be able to boast of a world-class education system. If they are to continue making a genuine contribution to the nation's well-being, independent schools must be allowed to maintain their independence. But independence does not mean isolation. Schools from both sectors must be prepared to work more closely together if they are to maximize the benefits they can offer to future generations of young people. For this fully to happen, it will require a preparedness to set aside some of the traditional suspicion and prejudices that exist on both sides. It will also require a greater appreciation on the government's part that independent schools contribute to the national good and that they are not somehow inimical to the interests of the country as a whole.

RUGBY SCHOOL

'WHITHER' (1936)

Hugh Lyon

Hugh Lyon imagines answering this question from an anxious parent: 'Pray, Mr. Head Master, how exactly do you propose to educate my son?' Today's Head Teachers are asked the same question all the time by prospective parents weighing up the claims of possible schools for their child. Seventy years ago, however, almost everything was taken on trust and the enquiry was a novelty. So Lyons suggests that Head Masters can be remarkably complacent, cocooned in their kingdoms, and specializing in self-congratulatory pronouncements on Speech Day. He takes a swipe at 'imperial fanatics, who would teach no history except that of the British Empire'; and he criticizes the vogue for teaching 'citizenship' which is 'being done elsewhere with frightening thoroughness': '.... the vigour and unanimity with which English teachers have revolted against such practices are at least not discreditable to our profession.'

Lyon sees the single end of education as 'the cultivation of a personality, not merely.... the greater efficiency of a body or a mind'. But he counters this with a word of caution:

The word 'character' has for long been the bug-bear of all who write about Public Schools. So many senseless cruelties and barbarisms have been defended by the assertion that they help to form character that it has been assumed that this claim will only be made for what is otherwise indefensible.

There has, Lyon says, been some development of the curriculum, but, 'It is something of a consolation, when we are perplexed with the competing claims of a multitude of subjects, to remember how little of what we teach will be remembered.... '. What will be remembered are the 'essential culture at the heart of every real subject of education' and 'that willingness to make mental effort, and that respect for both knowledge and for truth, which are the only hope of democracy'.

Lyon argues for a more formal approach to physical training – games, he says, are 'a splendid form of recreation.... but physically they do little more than exercise the limbs and keep muscles in good tone'. Art and Music are being given more attention, but the demands of 'necessary subjects', and the investment they require, means that often the best that can be done in these areas is to give the talented boy time, encouragement and skilled guidance.

However what is of crucial importance for Lyons is 'the education of the spirit' – something achieved most of all through personal example in the daily lives of Head Masters and teachers. So Lyon's aim for each boy in his charge is this – and it is worth quoting in full:

He should have a clear conception of the claims that others have upon him, in virtue both of his superior education and of his common humanity; and he should be on the look-out to meet these claims, in the sphere of social service, local government, parish or district clubs and societies. He should have a full understanding of his sexual powers and responsibilities, a high ideal of marriage, and a respect for women. In these days, too, no spiritual education is complete which has not given his sympathies a depth and a breadth undreamt-of in our fathers' time. The League of Nations, the awakening of India, the troubled aspirations of the neglected or the dissatisfied in every country under the sun, these demand not only a cool head but a warm heart. He will by rough-and-ready methods have learnt some social graces and have a natural leaning to unselfishness. He will esteem the more austere virtues, yet have found enjoyment and refreshment in the arts, and have many private rooms of his own into which he is happy to retire. Not afraid of responsibility, yet not over-anxious to assume it; resolute, intolerant of the false and the mean and the cruel; careless of popularity, yet overflowing with kindness of all things living; his hand stretched out to all men, his soul in constant communion with God. And still, let us hope, smiling as happily and trustfully as he did when he first shook hands with me.

TRANSFORMING LIVES

Patrick Derham

Recently I stumbled across the wonderful story of a party of American travellers in Mongolia in the 1980s, who in a remote corner of the Gobi Desert encountered a group of shaven monks from a primitive and isolated community who were crouched beside a small lake, and using its muddy waters for the purpose of kneading dough. Before they parted they taught the monks a jingle from an American advert and left them still at work all happily singing, 'Yo, Ho, Ho. We are the makers of Wonderbread'. The moral is clear. From time to time all of us in the world of education must stand back and reflect on what it is we are trying to do and ensure that we are not guilty of a similar delusion. None of us working in the independent sector can afford to be complacent or indolent, or operate in splendid isolation chanting, 'We are the makers of Wonderbread'. I fear though that there is an undeserved smugness and a feeling of superiority prevalent in some independent schools which does not reflect well on any of us in 2008. Yes, there are many things for us to trumpet and celebrate but equally there are too many challenges facing the independent sector for anyone to be sitting back thinking that the twenty-first century holds no fears.

A key challenge therefore is the necessity to recognize the dangers of complacency. Dr Arnold could not have put it better when he said this: 'There is nothing so unnatural and so convulsive to society as the strain to keep things fixed when all the world is in continual progress: and the cause of all the evils in the world may be traced to that natural but most deadly error of human indolence, that our business is to preserve and not to improve.... it is the ruin and fall alike of individuals, schools and nations.' This is as relevant for us in 2008 as it was when Arnold said it in the 1830s. Self-evaluation is crucial for the well-being of a great school and an effective Head has to encourage a culture that accepts the need for change. The dangers of complacency and smugness have to be avoided at all costs.

There should be no time for such an attitude, as the issue of our independence is one challenge that has stood the test of time. There remains a clear need for all Heads to work hard to demonstrate that the issue of our independence is not seen as a political issue. One way we can justify our independent status is to continue to show that our schools are not only healthy and vibrant but an enhancing feature within the community. Moreover, we need to show that our worth is demonstrated by the degree to which our pupils add to the sum total both of knowledge and happiness, and by the qualities of mind and judgment which they show, most especially in public life, and in a desire for the betterment of the world about them. Too often in the past independent schools, and indeed all schools, have been blamed for the ills and failings of society. Nonsense, of course, but we have to show by words and actions, rather than faith, if you like, that our contribution to the health of this country in the twenty-first century is as great as it was in Victorian times.

THE HEAD SPEAKS

I mention Victorian times because as a nineteenth century historian to be working in Dr Arnold's study at Rugby is a privilege. This is not the time to debate Arnold's influence but even his sternest critic has to recognize his singular contribution to the educational development of this country. Arnold in his time at Rugby encouraged Rugbeians to take their place in the world and to be aware of the world outside the school. For example, as I always remind my history sets here, we should not forget that Arnold's name was first on the petition of Rugby citizens on the subject of the Great Reform Act of 1832. Interestingly sitting on the bookshelf opposite my desk is a copy of the seventh edition of Arnold's lectures as Professor of History at Oxford; he only lived long enough to give one set of lectures as Professor of History. I am sure it was placed on the bookshelf deliberately many years ago for the education of his successors. During my first term I spent many happy hours reading the lectures; discovering such treasures as Arnold's description of the Siege of Genoa, which is said to have moved the then Master of Balliol to tears.

Though Arnold thought that the torch of civilization handed on from Greece to Rome and then on to Western Europe had not long to burn, he was in no doubt that we should use our experience and accumulated knowledge to progress even if man developed all too slowly in moral stature. 'Napoleon crossed the Alps,' he says, 'with scarcely the loss of a man, while Hannibal left behind him nearly half his Army: yet Napoleon was not a greater man than Hannibal nor was his enterprise conducted with greater ability. Two things we ought to learn from History: one that we are not in ourselves superior to our fathers; another, that we are shamefully and monstrously inferior to them if we do not advance beyond them'. All our schools have rich histories, and in many cases centuries of tradition, but the great schools are those that have built on those traditions, have a clear vision as to what it is they are trying to do in the modern world and a quiet air of confidence that what they are doing is for the greater good.

It is fair to say that Arnold was not a great fan of Lord Melbourne, Queen Victoria's first Prime Minister. I have always enjoyed this exchange between the young Queen and Melbourne at one of the early weekly audiences: 'I don't know, Ma'am, why they make all this fuss about education; none of the Pagets can read or write and they get on well enough'. It is fair to say that the independent sector has always made a fuss about education. In May 2007 I was in South Street Seaport in New York, and I visited the *Peking*, a four-masted barque built at the Blohm and Voss shipyard in Hamburg at the beginning of the twentieth century, which when owned by the Shaftesbury Homes, and moored on the River Medway at Lower Upnor in Kent, was my home and school for two years in the 1970s. Then it was known as the Training Ship *Arethusa* and as I stood on board so many memories filled my mind. I reflected on the lessons I had learnt there – valuable lessons about the importance of standing up for what is right and the benefits that stem from community life and the character development that flows naturally from activities outside of the classroom. Above all, though, as I stood on board I reflected on how different my life would have been if the ship had not closed in October 1974. I was being prepared for CSE Exams and the plan was that I would join the Navy at 16. Looking back at that time I had no knowledge of the public school system except what I had gleaned from the Jennings and

Darbyshire stories. My life was turned upside down when through charitable support I found myself at a school that offered me a whole new world of opportunities, similar to those enjoyed by the pupils in all our schools. In many ways I am living proof of that great nineteenth century Chartist slogan that 'Education is a liberating force'.

The idea of transforming lives being at the heart of a good education was brought home to me when I had lunch in May 2007 with George Horton, an 81-year-old Old Rugbeian, who lives in the USA. His story is worth sharing and he wrote in a recent book on Rugby (*With a Fine Disregard....*): 'I became a Rugbeian in the autumn of 1940 at the age of 14 – a pupil in Michell House. My family had escaped Nazi persecution in Germany in 1939, after my father's 1938 release from Sachsenhausen Concentration Camp. We arrived in England with 10 shillings in our pocket. This is when my mother wrote to Hugh Lyon, the Head Master of Rugby School, asking for help. Not merely did Mr Lyon accept me as a pupil at Rugby, but he also arranged for me to attend nearby Bilton Grange Prep School for a year.... I am sure that the fact that at the outbreak of the Second World War my father joined the British Expeditionary Force to France, having won the Iron Cross (first class) fighting for Germany in the First World War, played a role in this incredible act of generosity and humanity towards a poor, Jewish refugee family.... I soon found out that Rugby represented the opportunity of a lifetime.... (and) the depth and variety of a Rugby education was and continues to be a revelation.... Rugby for me was a haven and a springboard that I have never ceased to be grateful for'. A remarkable man, a remarkable story and one can understand why Hugh Lyon said in his 1945 Speech Day address that 'the more diverse the boys who enter into our heritage, the better'.

My experience, and the experience of George Horton, is far from unique. Many of our schools were founded with charitable intent and have throughout their history provided transformational opportunities for their pupils, advancing the cause of social mobility. For me, as for so many others, social mobility is not an abstract concept. It is what happened in my life primarily because of people who believed in me and who recognized the transforming nature of a good liberal education. My experience means I am passionately committed to giving every boy and girl the opportunity to dream dreams and to become, as Michael Gove (MP) expressed so powerfully, 'the authors of their own life stories'. We should not be shy in celebrating such stories of success. We should embrace the challenge posed by the Charities Act (2006) and in particular the public benefit test positively. We have nothing to fear and it is right and proper that in the twenty-first century we should all be working hard to broaden access to our schools.

This is important because I worry about the social exclusivity of our schools, particularly boarding schools. The spiralling fees (a 31% rise in the last five years) mean that the potential pool of pupils is inevitably diminishing. We all need to work hard to ensure that our intakes are as broad as possible and as far as possible a better reflection of the society of which all our pupils are part. So scholarships should be directed to those who need them and not given to the bright or talented children of the well-off. I was determined that we at Rugby should lead in this important respect and we were the first school to reduce all our scholarships to 10% in 2003 but at the same time to make all scholarships fully augmentable to 100% subject to means-testing. More schools need to follow and in time I suspect we will all be in a situation where scholarships carry no monetary reward at all. Rugby has had a longstanding provision for local children who can apply for support through the Lawrence Sheriff bequest but when I came to Rugby I wanted to create the same opportunities for boarding pupils. This is not the place to discuss the work of the Arnold Foundation but for me it fits naturally into a long-standing Rugby tradition, but one that is not unique to us. The important point to stress here is that all our fundraising is focused on providing transformational opportunities through the Arnold Foundation rather than on bricks and mortar.

Therein lies another challenge for our sector. For too long we have all been guilty of trying to outdo each other with ever improving facilities. A parent of a recent leaver wrote to me to say that it is interesting to think about what makes a school – banks of computers, playing fields, theatre facilities, art rooms and so on. His choice of school though was not based on this and perceptively he wrote: '…. so whilst a school probably has to have all the "toys" more importantly it is the ethos and feel of a place that makes it what it is'. How true that is and none of us must lose sight of the important lessons we are trying to pass on to those in our charge. Arthur fforde, a former Rugby Head Master, expressed it in a way that I think encapsulates what all of us believe. He said this in 1956: 'The criterion by which you judge …. a School like this one …. is not measurable in mechanical terms of statistics of victories or defeats, either in work or in play, or even by the achievements of its alumni.... The measure of it is in the air of the place, its attitudes, its energy, its humour, its seriousness, its courtesy, its conversability, its charity – the sense that, when one comes back to it in after years, one is coming back to a home of enduring things. It must, indeed, change in its outward aspect, adapting itself to a world that is changing all the time; but its inward essence, if it has got what it takes, is liable to stay unaltered, so that, when one comes back to it through long intervals of time, one still comes back to it as home'.

Traditionally great schools have defined their identity not by the prevailing madness of league tables, but by preserving and transmitting what Mathew Arnold said was 'the best that has been known and said in the world'. We should never forget this. We live in a world obsessed by testing and we run the risk of allowing our schools to become little more than efficient examination factories. We need to champion the values which can transform lives. We need to stand against the strait-jacket of the testing regime under which so many schools labour. We must point out the fallacy prevalent in government circles that we are on a continuum of academic improvement. We must speak out to say that preparing for too many tests and exams destroys the real purpose of education. We must have the confidence in what we are doing to get involved in influencing the curriculum debate on a national level to try and inject a modicum of sanity and realism. We must agitate for an exam system free from government interference.

Above all, though, we need to work hard to defend the importance of a broad liberal education. We need to stand up and proclaim the importance of developing a cultivated mind. The reason for this is crystal clear. In 1861 John Stuart Mill wrote in *Utilitarianism* that the cultivated mind 'finds sources of inexhaustible interest in all that surrounds it – the objects of nature, the achievements of art, the imagination of poetry, the incidents of history, the ways of mankind, past and present, and their prospects in the future'. In other words we should trumpet the fact that our raison d'être is the stimulation of the mind, the seeking of knowledge and the love of scholarship. This is not just for the purpose of exam results but, as Anthony Sutch argues, 'for the sake of life itself and living life to the full'.

I often use the story of Abraham Lincoln's educational experience to illustrate the importance of inculcating a love of learning and scholarship in our pupils. In 1858 Charles Lanman contacted all members of the US Congress for biographical details in order to prepare a Dictionary of Congress. Lincoln had not benefited from a formal education and when he reached the part of the questionnaire which asked for a list of his education he wrote one word: 'defective'. Lincoln had two brief experiences of school in an 'A.B.C. school' in Kentucky, but throughout his life he worked hard to become an educated person. I have always been struck by his determination to improve himself, for example in his teens he walked miles to borrow a book to educate himself further. Our pupils do not have a 'defective' education but we must ensure they develop the same passion and hunger that will be an enriching constant in their lives.

I have always been intrigued by the fact that Nehru, India's first Prime Minister, kept on his desk these lines written by the American poet Robert Frost:

> The woods are lovely, dark and deep
> But I have promises to keep,
> And miles to go before I sleep,
> And miles to go before I sleep.

Nehru passionately believed, as I do, that motivation is more important than ability. The importance of working hard at a particular task and learning from our failures as well as our successes is all important. Too many of today's pupils are products of an upbringing where the word 'No' is not used enough and where parents operate on the basis that life shouldn't contain anything that makes us unhappy. If a school is preparing young people for life – and it is – it would be wrong to give young people the impression that life is devoid of pain and it is wrong to give adolescents the impression that in life you don't have to get along with people you don't like or perform tasks that are difficult or unpleasant. A few years ago I was taken aback when a member of the School's Levee (prefect) told me that she did not like to take risks as her most common fear was the fear of failure. She felt anxious about attempting something unless she knew she could succeed at it. We are not doing our job if we do not teach our pupils that failure can teach us more than success and that without risks parts of us go entirely unused. Theodore Roosevelt put it very well when he said:

> It is not the critic who counts, nor the man or woman who

points out where the strong stumbled or where the doer of deeds could have done them better. The credit belongs to the people who are actually in the arena. At best they know the triumph of big achievement; if they fail, at least they fail while doing greatly, so that their place shall never be with those cold and timid souls who know neither victory nor defeat.

All of us involved in education would agree with Dr Jex-Blake's remark at the end of his reply to the Resident Fellows of Cambridge in 1879. 'You cannot create genius,' he wrote, 'but you can encourage good teaching'. There is a continuing challenge for us all to encourage those who are passionate about their subjects to work in our schools and to enjoy imparting that excitement and passion in the young. The virtue of independence is a freedom from some of the bureaucracy that plagues the wider educational world but the curse of regulation is here to stay for us all. We must though not see the spark crushed in the young teacher. We must encourage risk taking. We must ensure that our staff cajole, entice and impel our young onwards and upwards and so will be remembered in years to come by grateful pupils. Peter Hall put it very well when he said of his experience of his school days that 'Education is not so much a matter of which school you go to…. it is more whether you have the good fortune to meet two or three special teachers who light up your mind and encourage your spirit'. We must all strive to nurture these 'special teachers' who are crucial in the quest to transform lives, teachers who, as Constantine Cavafy wrote in his magnificent poem *Ithaca*, show the pupils in their charge 'that the road is long, full of adventure, full of knowledge'.

All of us would subscribe to these sentiments and all of us fervently believe in the importance of community which not only underpins our society but enriches life itself. All of us too, even on the occasional difficult day, must never lose sight of the privileged position we have to work with the young and the opportunity we have been given really to make a difference. Another book on the bookshelf opposite my desk is the 1897 biography of Arnold written by Findlay. One sentence at the beginning of the chapter on School Life at Rugby makes me smile: 'It would be useless to give any chronological details of a life so necessarily monotonous as that of the Headmaster of a public school'. How untrue that is. It is a wonderful job, full of challenges and frustrations, but ultimately a job that is both enriching and fulfilling.

So what is it, ultimately, that makes a school, and what have we been striving for – or should we be striving for – in our schools? The answer partly emerges when one thinks of the contribution of people within the institution, because schools are about the people in them and not the systems that operate. What is of supreme importance in our schools is I think easy to identify. It is more than good academic work or lively activity in the arts and in games. It is more than inspiring Services in Chapel, or links with local schools and the local community, or involvement in the wider concerns of the world. These are certainly symptoms of the spirit which should pervade a school and of course they are important. But how, in the first place, does one learn to commit oneself; to trust rather than fear, to build rather than destroy?

The answer in my view lies in a deep respect for each individual –

boy or girl, pupil or member of staff. Groups are important, whether in family or school; but groups really only confirm and spread what is already happening at the level of individuals. If there is care in personal relationships and people have time for each other, and bear with each other's faults, the group takes on a warmth and confidence. But groups reflect and reinforce the opposite qualities just as quickly: the problems that are so evident in wider society today have their small counterpart in a casual insult thrown across a study passage, or indifference shown to the boy or girl who doesn't quite fit in. No community can be immune from this kind of thing.

But what I want to see in any school that I am involved with is the willingness of the staff, and of the boys and girls, to engage with each other at a personal level, since this is the only way that good relationships are fostered and bad ones mended. It is this spirit, this respect of person for person, based as it is on the Christian view of human value, which makes Rugby (and all our schools) so rewarding a place in which to live and work.

ST PAUL'S SCHOOL

'Aims and Problems' (1936)

John Bell

With Hitler's Germany casting a shadow over Europe, John Bell reflects on the difficulty of educating children in such uncertain times, and on the dangers of political and economic nationalism:

Almost everyone will agree that, in the future, there must either be an increase of political and economic nationalism, which must inevitably lead to conflict and the end of the civilization in which we have been brought up ourselves, or a wider understanding and co-operation between the different nations which in the past have clung passionately to their separate ideals and ways of life.

In a rapidly changing world, perhaps the best that can be done is to 'ensure that, whatever the future may have in store, our sons and daughters may be able, through character and training, to avoid disaster and achieve happiness for themselves and their own children'.

Bell complains about the over-specialized curriculum, which may suit the boy destined for honours at a university, but leaves the needs of those of average intelligence – and the late-developer – unfulfilled.

For these boys, the studying of commercial geography, contemporary history, a foreign language ('studied as it is spoken and written today'), economics, law and statistics is more appropriate. But he rightly concludes that, 'The personality and methods of the teacher matter much more than the details of such a curriculum. After all, he argues (in a vein that runs through both <u>The Head Master Speaks</u> and <u>The Head Mistress Speaks</u>), it is important to train boys to think for themselves so that they see through 'slogans and advertisements' and can 'debunk the charlatans and sentimentalists whose influence upon public opinion can be so disastrous in the modern world'.

In spite of his demand for a more relevant curriculum for the majority of pupils, Bell maintains that it is not the role of schools to teach the specialized skills required in business, any more than they should train lawyers, doctors or engineers. However he proposes a system of part-time education up to the age of eighteen which will combine the best of both secondary and technical curricula.

Bell warns of the 'danger that examinations may become an incubus upon the life of a school, stifling natural growth or producing hot-house plants that flourish for a time but wither when exposed to the open air'. In what might be a comment on the current pernicious League Tables, he writes:

An imposing list of scholarship successes, or of Higher and School Certificates, merely indicates that the school contains a number of able boys, or has an efficient teaching staff; it may be a rough guide to parents that work takes first place, but it does not guarantee that their sons will go out into the world fully equipped in every direction to make the best of their opportunities, and to play a useful part in the life of their country or their town.

It is appropriate that in 2008 St. Paul's has taken the decision not to provide information for League Tables.

Finally Bell turns his attention briefly to Physical Education:

Schools will in future have to devote more time and attention to the general building up of sound constitutions than to the coaching of a minority of natural athletes.

To teacher-training:

The problem of the proper training of teachers has not yet been solved; it is unreasonable to suppose that a young man of twenty-three, who has just taken his degree, should be qualified without further study to undertake one of the most difficult of jobs.

And most importantly to religion:

....those who teach and those who learn in any school must have some ideal, some aim in life higher and more lasting than material prosperity or the pursuit of pleasure, if their school is to serve any good purpose.... where there is no vision, the people perish.

A VIEW FROM THE HAMMERSMITH BRIDGE

Martin Stephen

Seventy years ago my predecessor John Bell worried about a curriculum that was too narrow, the need to teach young people to think for themselves, the importance of getting young people interested in politics and the dominance of examinations. His world was one where the financial heart had been torn out of an Imperial nation that could no longer afford its Empire, where its brightest and best young people had been decimated in the First World War, where the deepest economic depression in history was affecting all the industrialized world and where the growing tide of Fascism was rising like a poisonous black cloud to cover Europe and threaten the world. It seems a very different world, and it is interesting to compare the view from Hammersmith Bridge seventy years on.

I could not agree less with Bell about the need for a broader curriculum. In terms of how we manage the curriculum we have managed to get just about everything wrong, including making the compulsory curriculum far too broad, the choices within it far too narrow. The pendulum has swung so far the other way as to smash through the casing of the clock and get stuck there. We have concentrated on designing an overall curriculum but spent far less time on the equally important issue of the quality and depth of knowledge a teacher has of the subjects he or she delivers through that curriculum. We feel we have achieved something when every child in the UK is committed to studying Maths up to the age of sixteen, whilst the whole noble vision is undermined by the fact that only 40% of Maths teachers in the UK have a degree or equivalent qualification in Maths. We have failed to meet basic standards in core subjects in that curriculum whilst expanding the number of subjects massively. We have shifted a whole load of society's conscience on to that curriculum, making teachers and schools more and more responsible for preaching against drug misuse, teenage pregnancy and a host of other problems—in effect, we have sought to replace the Vicar of the Established Church by the teacher in the Educational Establishment. We have included in our curriculum a host of new examination subjects that are not acceptable by Russell Group universities, nor favoured by employers. We have taught more and more, without apparently teaching it any better. Was John Bell too successful in his pleading for a broader curriculum? I know that the happiest day of my life was waking up at a school I hated and feeling happy for almost the first time because I knew that at the advanced age of sixteen I would never have to attend another Maths lesson in my life. English, History and Geography at A-level – hopelessly narrow in modern terms – released me to do what I did and enjoyed best, yet I am now a heretic for saying so and preaching against the over-broad curriculum at 16+. It appears it would be better for me to have done two more years of Maths and Science that I had no interest in and which I would never use, and cut down on my English and History, a main attraction of which was to go into my subject in wonderful depth.

Where John Bell was right was that not every child needs or benefits from an academic curriculum. What has gone wrong is the change in this to an entirely different concept: no child will have a solely academic curriculum. It is treated as if it were blasphemy, but is it actually so wrong to claim that a child in the top 15% of the ability band who wishes to go to a research university to read Maths, Physics or whatever, benefits hugely by being given a rather special, albeit restricted diet? We tried to answer this problem with grammar schools, but all we did was condemn 70% of children to sump schools, a recipe for a revolution that duly came with comprehensivization. What we should do is allow any child access to a fast-track class in any subject at any age, where due talent is shown, and then reinvent the old School Leaving Certificate—a basic guarantee of core skills—at the age of fourteen. Thereafter the child should be allowed to choose an academic or a vocational path, or seek to mix and match. No child should be refused admission to the academic stream, but to continue on in it they should be required to meet minimum, examined or tested standards. If at the end of a year they fail to jump that hurdle, they should be allowed to repeat each and any year which they fail.

I do not agree with John Bell that teaching young people to think for themselves is a major priority for our age. I agree it is an essential skill for a young person: I am far from convinced we need to teach it. Here the situation has improved in leaps and bounds since Bell's day. The 30's were far more authoritarian than the present day, dictating to young people what they should think on a wide range of issues. Our liberal attitudes are a threat to the weak on occasion, leaving them vulnerable to the loudest voice, but the invention of the teenager, a revolution in personal and uncensored communication through the internet, voting at eighteen and a host of other social changes mean that our young people are arguably the most independent thinkers our society has ever produced. This process has been hastened by the declining number of agencies that used to dictate what young people thought, or at least claimed that right: Government, schools, the Church or an old-style patriarchal employer.

The need to get young people interested in politics is as important as ever. In the absence of the young involving themselves in politics, they get the rulers they deserve. Our problem is that we have reviled politicians so much as to make them dirty in the eyes of young people, whose involvement has as a result gravitated towards Greenpeace or the battle against global warming. To add to young people's distrust of politics, the environment is perhaps the most notable area in which politics has failed to make any real impact.

And how about the dominance of exams? Turn in your grave, John Bell. Our children are more tested (weighing the pig not fattening it) than ever before in our history. The examination and qualification industry has become just that, either a wholly-owned Government subsidiary or a self-perpetuating oligarchy. Those who mark exams frequently have no contact with the end-user of those qualifications (universities and employers), and there is a massive crisis in recruiting markers. We are set on destroying A-level but have nothing to replace it, and have failed miserably to come up with credible vocational qualifications. It is not just that we are more and more dominated by tests and exams, but also that those tests and exams are increasingly flawed and unable to bear the weight we put upon them. The combination of a compulsory national curriculum and the importance attached to test and exam results has certainly acted to take at least some of the fun out of teaching: nothing could take *all* the fun out of teaching. There is less time for teachers to gather flowers by the wayside, less time to divert a lesson onto a special passion or interest of a pupil and less capacity to experiment or be innovative in one's teaching style.

Yet examinations have taken on an even more sombre tone than John Bell could have dreamt of in his worst nightmares. The league tables are a cancer on the face of education. They favour hugely schools which are selective. They have encouraged schools to make their students sit for 'soft' subjects, at the expense of subjects such as Maths, English and the Sciences. They have generated commercially-driven exams which have the selling point of racking up a school's points score at GCSE. They have encouraged schools to 'cull' their sixth forms so as to maximize numbers of A and B grades. They sell newspapers, and because of this editors are encouraged to find new ways of manipulating the figures so as to make 'interesting' schools come top. They are increasingly a statistical lie. The International Baccalaureate receives a wholly disproportionate points score from UCAS, giving undue and unearned prominence in the league tables to schools who enter for this examination. They do not recognize International GCSE, or IGCSE, despite that examination being widely recognized as more demanding than GCSE. One result is that when St Paul's switched to IGCSE, its performance as recorded in the official Government league tables sank from a 100% success rate to a 1%

success rate. Had IGCSE been included, the figure would have remained at 100%.

It was a mixed bag for John Bell, I think: one arrow in the bull's eye, one on the target and two lost in the shrubbery behind the range. Seventy years on, I hope someone is as kind about me, but I doubt it. As for my own challenges and visions....

Challenges

Every book ever produced to help people take an Assembly has a quotation stating that the young are worthless, have no respect for their elders and waste their time in useless activity and then credits it to Seneca or someone who lived a very long time ago. Have we always faced a crisis in educating our young people? I suspect that no society has got it completely right, and many have got it completely wrong. Yet there is a current sense, be it right or wrong, that we are in quite a severe crisis at present, and face unusually harsh challenges.

We face a real crisis in academic education. We have refused to accept that the most able in our society are a special-needs category. We have failed to recognize the fact that peer-group pressure, especially in schools where the average family has no aspirations towards university, can exterminate academic ambition, just as bright children, if concentrated together, achieve critical mass, strike sparks and make the sum of the parts greater than the whole. We have concentrated on how much the bright child can pull up the standard for the less gifted, been too frightened to admit how much the weak child can ham-string the able one.

At the other end of the spectrum, we have failed to improve the lot of the underclass, the children who gain no qualifications, no love of or respect for learning and no hope from their schooldays. We have fed them a GCSE examination that is too boring to appeal to many of those most able, yet too difficult to be attainable by and hence give a sense of achievement to the least able.

We have failed to attract enough top graduates into teaching. One reason is that we are addicted to a view of the teacher as a generalist, equally at ease with preparing pupils for Oxbridge and helping a special needs pupil understand some Science. Some teachers can do both; many cannot. With a massive increase in house prices and a savage increase in student debt we have failed to recognize the crucial need to supply subsidized housing to new teachers, particularly in deprived or expensive inner-city and suburban areas.

We have failed to support schools in their imposition of discipline, making it too easy for decisions to be overturned. We have also made it too easy for false allegations to be made against teachers, prolonged the outcome of hearings and allowed teachers to be tried and destroyed by media and community pressure long before they are tried by law.

We have never defined coherently what a school is, and have allowed nineteen separate types or category of school to exist in the UK, namely:

11 – 16 Comprehensive Schools
11 – 18 Comprehensive Schools

Maintained Grammar Schools

Middle Schools

City Technology Colleges

City Academies

Voluntary-Aided Schools

Voluntary-Controlled Schools

Faith Schools

Foundation Schools

Community Schools

Village Colleges

Maintained Boarding Schools

Sixth Form Colleges

Further Education Colleges (educating 16-18 year-old pupils)

Specialist Schools

All-girl High Schools

Pupil Referral Units

Independent Schools

We have failed to make examination marking a respectable or desirable career option.

We have allowed ourselves to become locked in a sterile debate over selection, a war of attrition based now more on dogma, political fundamentalism, class and the politics of envy than on any real and meaningful educational values. We have allowed a crucial human right – freedom of opportunity – to be transmuted into the mantra that all children must be offered the same opportunity, regardless of their gifts and talents.

THE HEAD SPEAKS

We have allowed crucial areas of activity, most notably music, drama and competitive sport, to lapse in too many schools, sometimes for funding reasons, sometimes because of shortage of staff, sometimes because of the withdrawal of goodwill by teachers and sometimes because of a suffocating Health and Safety regime. These activities are leaders in educating children in two crucial life skills, team membership and risk management, as well as vital to the success of the sporting and cultural life of the country.

We have made university education vastly expensive at the point of sale, yet starved universities of proper funding. We have mounted a massive expansion in university education based on the rather vague idea that 'it is good for as many people to go to university as possible', yet we never costed it out, assessed the employment implications for thousands of graduates in 'soft' subjects or bothered to define what a university is and what purpose it should serve. We have allowed a three-tier university system to occur: Ivy League, Red Brick and New, with only a very few crossovers, and large numbers of students attending colleges that are not highly regarded by employers and which carry no bonus in the jobs market. We have saddled students with over £20,000 of debt, and justified this on higher-earning figures for graduates based on the time when far fewer people went to university. Like someone allowing genetically-modified material out into the biosphere without proper testing, we have not evaluated the impact of this burden of debt on, for example, the ability of young people to put down a deposit on a house or recruitment into the traditionally low-paid but essential social services.

There is another major challenge looming for our universities. The logical answer for many of the top twenty or so UK universities is to take more and more overseas students. There is every reason, from their viewpoint, to do so. They earn far more from overseas students, whose fees are not capped, and the leading universities tend to attract the cream of overseas students who often have very high level skills in Maths and other core subjects. This means less demand for remedial work in the first year at university, or even a need for degree courses that last a year less than some do at present. Figures such as 'only 25% of our undergraduate intake will come from the UK in ten years time' are being bandied around Senior Common Rooms. It cannot be right to exclude that proportion of candidates whose only crime is to hold a UK passport.

Visions

The first vision is for the country to arrive at a genuine, nationally-observed pattern for secondary education. The splintered nature of our present system is bad for resourcing and bad for training, as well as being bewilderingly confusing. We have allowed different types of school to be bolted on to our system in a manner similar to scientists who bolt on an extra module to a Soyuz space vehicle. It is time we decided a truly national and unified maintained education system. The Australian system, with its overall coherence, ability to offer some regional independence, and capacity to run the public and private sectors alongside each other productively should be a starting point.

A solution to the debate over selection is to create the choice of an academic or vocational pathway at the age of fourteen, and allow unrestricted entry into either pathway for the first year of study, together with the ability to re-sit years where minimum standards had not been reached by the end of the year.

We must design a new set of vocational qualifications designed essentially by employers and resource these, including a major resurrection of apprenticeship schemes. The proposals of the Tomlinson report, suitably adapted, should be adopted. A School Leaving Certificate should be introduced at the age of fourteen as a gatekeeper to further education and as a guarantor of basic standards.

We need to create a new career path of Chartered Examiner. This should be available by full or part-time study, and the job be undertaken on a full or part-time basis.

We must involve universities and employers far more closely in the examinations that select or qualify people for their sector, create a single examining board for the UK freed from any imperative to be profit-making, and de-politicize QCA to make it far more independent of Government and representative of universities, employers and the teaching profession.

The structure of secondary education in the UK should be designed by a politically independent standing commission, the dominant majority of which would consist of universities and employers.

The importance of subject disciplines should be emphasized anew in secondary teaching. A specialism in teaching the gifted and talented should be established. Sixth Form Colleges should be encouraged to relate strongly to and be involved with 11-16 schools.

To improve the quality of teaching in the UK we should:

- Offer subsidized housing to young teachers.
- Pay off student debt for those who satisfactorily complete five years of teaching.
- Utilize more fully the talents of older pupils by using them as mentors.
- Utilize the skills of mature graduates who might wish to transfer into teaching for the last ten years or so of their working lives.
- Increase the penalties for those making false accusations against teachers.

As for universities, we need to define or even re-define what a university is and what it is meant to do with and for its students. Is it an organization dedicated to research and to educating the academically most able? Is it an organization destined to ease the path of young people into what Bell's age might have called 'trade and commerce'? Is it simply a way of keeping young people off the streets? Alongside that, we need to decide just how many university graduates the country needs and can afford, and in what subjects. We might also look at the high-earning and profit-making areas such as banking, the law and the City who rely on graduate recruitment to pay more towards the universities who supply them with their lifeblood.

There is also the issue of the challenges facing the independent sector, and what its vision should be. Though it is not a popular view, it is likely that independent education is facing the biggest crisis in its history. Ironically, that crisis comes about because independent education has never been so successful. 61.8% of A* grades in single-subject Science are now achieved by the 7% of pupils in independent schools. At A-level, over a third of A grades in Science subjects are gained by independent sector pupils. Despite massive efforts made by the sector to widen access by making more and more bursary places available, the sector's success makes it more desirable, whilst it is still unaffordable by many parents. A major, and usually unreported, factor is that since the abolition of the Direct Grant Schools in 1976 there has been no tradition of easy, subsidized access to high-quality academic education in the UK. Put bluntly, we now have in the UK large numbers of parents who simply do not believe that a place at an independent school is a viable proposition for them or their child. This makes the sector even more prone to the politics of envy. Its success rubs salt into the wounds of particularly a left-wing government, whilst New Conservatism cannot be seen to be too closely associated with the sector in case it labels it as Old Conservatism. The vision is as clear as it is demanding: a move on the part of the sector to raise massive new endowment funds, with a view to the schools becoming needs-blind as regards entry.

Another vision for the sector is the growth of real partnership schemes between the independent and the maintained sector. Too many existing schemes are cursory, photogenic and fail to address the real strengths of the sector. This vision is clouded by political correctness. Of course the independent sector cannot go round to the maintained sector as did the Squire's Lady in times past, distributing largesse to the educational poor of the parish in a patronizing way, and of course there are many superb maintained schools. Yet the fact remains that the independent sector can teach the maintained sector at least some things about teacher recruitment and retention, about getting the best out of the most able, about competitive and team sport, music and drama. These are the strengths of the independent schools, and these are what they can most usefully export. Yet there is no workable financial model to allow this to happen, and without Government subsidy the sector faces serious resistance from parents who are paying twice over for education and who do not see why their fees should subsidize maintained schools for the third time.

To conclude, then, the challenge facing us at the moment is confusion: confusion about what education is for, and confusion about what form the institutions that deliver it should take. We lack an overall philosophy of education, and suffer from a hybrid, muddled amalgam that in seeking to be all things to all people gives too many of them too little. And as for vision …? We do not really have a vision for education in the UK, nor does there seem to be anyone who can supply us with it.

STOWE SCHOOL

'THE PUBLIC SCHOOLS AND THE FUTURE' (1936)

J. F. Roxburgh

Stowe was only thirteen-years-old when J. F. Roxburgh, its founding Headmaster, contributed to The Head Master Speaks. Although Roxburgh admits to founding Stowe on the model of a public school, he nevertheless questions the model and wonders whether it is destined to survive much longer.

Public schools, he argues, are essentially boarding schools, popular as much for their convenience as for their quality. They serve the 'upper middle classes' who cannot find secondary education close to their home – and by being educated at country boarding schools, boys enjoy peace and spaciousness that they would not find in a town school. But Roxburgh rightly foresees that improved transport will soon lead to the growth of day schools: 'Ultimately the Country will be able to do without boarding schools if it wishes to'.

Roxburgh goes on to make the case against boarding schools ('a case little understood by those who have personal reasons for loving one of them'). In boarding schools, he argues, boys are in such close contact with each other that they are educated in their most impressionable years more by other boys than by adults, missing the influence of parents and their friends at home. The 'moral and intellectual atmosphere' of a boarding school is determined by the majority of its pupils, and so it tends to be conventional and comfortable, with opinions shaped by common-place and juvenile ideas: the minority of 'clever' and 'vigorous' boys are disadvantaged by living 'for months at a time among companions as little developed as himself'. The problem is compounded by the fact that many boarding school masters themselves become 'permanently juvenile.... arrested adolescents'. Thus although boys know their masters better than boys in day schools, they still 'lack the influence of truly adult adults'. While the case for the coeducational boarding school is not yet proved, boarding schools are 'monastic' institutions where boys 'see so little of their feminine contemporaries that to a few of them a woman will seem a remote and unreal creature for years afterwards'.

But Roxburgh acknowledges that boarding school has its advantages too, especially since (helped by the newer foundations) it is 'progressively modernizing, liberating and humanizing itself'. By sending them to boarding school, busy and often overworked parents are freed from the responsibility of looking after their adolescent sons and hand it to the experts. Rebellious teenagers can kick out at school authority rather than against parental authority, 'into which emotion always enters' (though with more space at school there is perhaps less provocation to kick out in the first place). Boys will 'learn.... to live with other people.... to assume as normal and necessary a high standard of conduct.... to be loyal to a community which has.... high implicit ideals of manhood'. Moreover boarding schools satisfy the desire of most boys to 'live with other boys and be brought up with them'. They have 'teams to play for or applaud, with a House.... to support and with rival Houses to execrate'. When a boy becomes older, 'the school provides him with subordinates to manage and with an institution he can not only serve, but love'.

Finally Roxburgh comments on two specific problems faced by the Public Schools. First, he considers the fact that schoolboys now mature earlier than previously, and since the school leaving age has remained unchanged [the pressure was in fact to raise it from fourteen to fifteen] the result is 'an annual crop of arrested adolescents'. Roxburgh's solution is that boys should leave Public School at seventeen rather than eighteen and spend a year travelling abroad, or gain experience in 'works.... or in an office'. Secondly he suggests that boarding schools must make themselves more accessible to entrants from state primary schools – which will mean somehow bridging the gap between the transfer in the state system from primary to secondary school at age eleven and the traditional public school entry at age thirteen. Public Schools, says Roxburgh,

.... will only justify their existence if they prove both willing and worthy to receive all the best boys born in England and to make the most that can be made of them. The alternative is the creation of ever more and ever better day-schools, to which, as transport improves, boys of all sorts will go, until the Public Schools, famous but unwanted, will fade gradually away, having failed to grasp the greatest opportunity for service ever offered them.

IF...

Anthony Wallersteiner

Independent schools have always shown a remarkable capacity for reinventing themselves. While many of the great public schools trace their origins to the dissolution of the monasteries or earlier, they generally remained modest establishments until the coming of the railways, the emergence of an aspirational middle class with enough wealth to pay fees and the urgent need for nurseries to mould colonial administrators and supervisors to serve in the furthest outposts of empire.

Traditions were invented which soon acquired the patination of being time-honoured: patriotic paeans to English youth were penned as school songs; crests and shields bore Latin exhortations to put honour and duty above self-interest; crocketed gables and crenellated towers looked back to a golden age of nationhood in the making. Now, when every glossy school prospectus proclaims the virtues of independent thinking, personal freedoms and pastoral care for each and every pupil, the length of time that the Victorian and Edwardian model of public school education held sway is easily forgotten. As recently as the late 1960s all but a few of the public schools condoned fagging, corporal punishment and churned out stereotypical automatons who believed in their own innate superiority and took pride in sharing the same codes, habits and beliefs. Individuality and sensitivity were discouraged with sneering disdain as pupils were conditioned to "play up! play up! and play the game!"

As the maintained sector rushed headlong into the experiment of comprehensivization in the 1960s and 1970s, the public schools seized the opportunity to remould themselves by modernizing and humanizing their conventions and surroundings. Idiosyncracies and eccentricities were no longer frowned upon as dangerous manifestations of potentially subversive behaviour. Pupils were taught to respect and consider the needs of others while developing interests and skills to the best of their ability. A new liberalism and culture of tolerance and social responsibility swept through the public schools in response to the political, cultural and social upheavals of the late 1960s. No longer was being bad at games a one-way ticket to social ostracism and the misery inflicted on those who would not or could not conform was consigned to the dustbin of history. The iconoclastic film 'If', released in 1968, celebrates the dramatic passing of the ancien regime in Britain's public schools. By the mid-1970s dormitories were being converted into study bedrooms, communal showers and bathrooms turned into private cubicles and morally dubious staff whose sexual proclivities had been tolerated for years were quietly moved on or persuaded to retire.

Models of capitalist Darwinism, the private sector responded to market forces in the Thatcherite 1980s by outstripping expenditure on state schools and investing in elaborate facilities for art, drama, music, and sport. Staff were trained to vary their teaching styles while language laboratories, departmental audio-visual libraries and, more recently, whole-school ICT networks transformed the delivery of the curriculum. Dyslexia, dyspraxia, attention deficit disorder and dyscalculia began to be recognized as valid conditions which require specialist knowledge of different learning and processing abilities. Many schools appointed Special Educational Needs coordinators and some opened Skills Development Centres to provide individual tuition and bespoke learning. A plethora of subjects from Astronomy to Mandarin and sports as diverse as Clay Pigeon Shooting and Wake Boarding cater to the tastes of a more cosmopolitan clientele who shop around without any great attachment or loyalty to the old school tie. Crucially, however, the public schools maintain tried and tested teaching methods based on high expectations, small classes (an average ratio of one teacher for every 9.3 pupils compared with 17.1 in state schools), setting by ability, effective management and firm discipline. Subject specialists are recruited to draw out talents and fire up the will-o'-the-wisp of enthusiasm which will often burn brightly for many years to come.

The benefits of this strategy are clear: the best teachers make difficult topics intelligible and encourage inquisitive pupils to challenge conventional orthodoxies by going outside the straitjacket of the curriculum. All pupils have capacity to respond to and benefit from higher academic expectations relative to their ability. They can escape the tick-box culture of mechanistic exam assessments if teachers acquaint them with 'the best that has been known or said in the world and thus with the history of the human spirit' (Matthew Arnold). Without wider reading, love of subject, intellectual risk taking, experiment and research, how will the next generation of scientists be inspired to push ahead in state-of-the-art diagnostics, robotic surgery or stem cell research? How will geographers penetrate the truth behind the headlines on global warming and prophecies of environmental catastrophe? Historians need to be taught that although the past is another country, it was once inhabited by Greeks and Romans, Vikings and Visigoths, Lancastrians and Yorkists, Roundheads and Cavaliers, Jacobites and Hanoverians, Fascists and Communists, men and women, as real as we are today, with their own ideas, passions, hopes and disappointments. Music, Art and Literature celebrate beauty and truth, creativity and imagination, and lead us to a deeper understanding of the human condition. We should not underestimate the value of a cultural hinterland which allows us to transcend the here and now of an egotistical age worshipping at the altar of shallow materialism (Marx's 'fetishistic character of commodities').

Ambition, traduced as a vice by supporters of a more egalitarian system, is the handmaiden of success in schools which place a high value on the pursuit of academic excellence. Trial and error is seen as the best way of learning from mistakes in a system which rejects the fantastical notion that All Must Have Prizes. Genuine achievements are celebrated in weekly assemblies, prize-givings, scholarships and university honours boards which hang prominently in libraries, corridors and dining rooms. The idea of belonging to an elite – a word used pejoratively in some circles – is not discouraged if this means the promotion of the best scientists, linguists, mathematicians and students of humanities. The result of this strategy is the disproportionate over-representation of the public schools at the top of the annual league tables and in winning places at the selecting Russell Group universities – particularly on degree courses in Chemistry, Physics, Mathematics, Classics and Modern Languages, which require a considerable amount of advanced specialist knowledge.

Reports of the imminent demise of boarding schools have also been much exaggerated – in spite of eye-watering fee increases and demographic decline. Seventy years ago, J. F. Roxburgh (the first Head Master of Stowe), fretted that the increasing number of good day schools and the stultifying and oppressive conservatism of boys and staff in single-sex boarding schools would lead to the fading away of the 'famous but unwanted' public schools. JF need not have worried: these days few pupils 'emigrate' to boarding schools for three month stretches at a time to become 'naturalized' on arrival. Modern boarding schools complement families rather than replace them. Exeats, half-terms, frequent parental visits and a steady flow of communications have reduced the impact of separation from home without diminishing the sense of belonging to a community. Time saved in not having to commute to and from school on a daily basis can be spent in the pursuit of a talent such as practising the violin, perfecting a drop kick, researching a coursework assignment on Baudelaire or simply chatting to friends.

While pockets of boorishness may still exist and there may be a few masters 'whose minds are permanently juvenile', an enlightened revolution has transformed the experience of twenty-first century boarding. Tolerance, self-restraint, common sense and trust are nurtured in caring and supportive environments in which pastoral care is provided by teams of housemasters, tutors, matrons and counsellors. Roxburgh worried that the artificiality of the single-sex boarding school might distort relationships and attitudes in later life. These days all but a handful of boarding schools have embraced co-education and equality between the sexes with a vigour which would have been shocking only a generation ago. There is widespread recognition that co-educational boarding confers a subtle and almost intangible emotional intelligence and sensitivity which prepares pupils to live and work together in an increasingly complex, pluralist and competitive adult world.

The Independent Schools Council lists 509,000 children as being educated in private schools – 40,000 more than when Labour came to power in 1997 with the promise that 'education, education, education' would be the government's number one priority. In spite of spending on state schools reaching £77.4 billion a year, an increase by two thirds in real terms since 1997, value for money has been disappointing. Targets and league tables have squeezed out inspiration and the promise of intellectual excitement in the classroom by reducing our schools to little more than joyless factories which measure education in tests and exam scores in the same way that units of car production or barrels of oil measure output in industry. With external assessments at seven, eleven, fourteen, sixteen, seventeen and eighteen, pupils in British state schools have the unenviable distinction of being the most heavily examined in the world – with the possible exception of the North Koreans. In spite of this obsession with tests and tables, only 46% of pupils in state schools achieve five or more GCSEs at grades A* to C. There are 639 state secondary schools, one in five, where fewer than 30% of pupils obtain five or more good grade passes at GCSE, including Maths and English. The Pisa Study, published in November 2007 by the Organization for Economic Co-operation and Development, reveals that standards of achievement in Reading, Science and Maths among Britain's fifteen-year-olds have slumped since the previous survey in 2001. Britain now languishes twenty-third in the OECD's league table of thirty countries – behind Greece, Hungary and Ireland – with only Turkey showing a wider attainment gap between its state and private schools.

The unremitting and ultimately unsuccessful drive to impose centralized policies on schools makes it clear that the greatest determinant of quality in education is not money but independence. The resourcefulness and popularity of the private schools should be a spur to emulation by the maintained sector. Independent schools are fortunate in having their own inspectorate (although this is now under threat) and in being able to ignore many of the edicts which pour out of the department for Children, Schools and Families. Private schools can focus on building communities based on evolving values in which membership comes from parents who know the needs of their children better than the state. Everyone agrees that educational standards must improve if Britain is to compete with the emerging giants of India and China. Unfortunately, too much time has been wasted on politically motivated attacks when the independent sector should be applauded for saving the tax payer £2.2 billion a year and for setting high standards in every sphere of school life.

A more creative solution to solving the ills of social inequality and ending Britain's educational apartheid would be to open up the independent sector to a broader swathe of the population by issuing vouchers equivalent to the value of the cost of educating a child in a state school. These vouchers could be redeemed at any school – giving parents the right to choose freely what is best for their children; schools would actively compete for pupils and there would be an influx of new providers (charities, community groups, universities, venture capitalists) into the educational market place. Greater competition would bring fees down and standards would rise as dissatisfied parents could vote with their feet by transferring their allegiances to another school. Children in areas of economic deprivation could be given vouchers worth more than those given to the young growing up in areas of leafy affluence. Social mobility, frozen with the abolition of all but 164 grammar schools, would be miraculously restored with much wider access to an education hitherto only available to about 8% of the school population.

Evidence for the success of state funded private schools can be found in Sweden, Holland and the American cities of Milwaukee and Cleveland. City academies are a step in the right direction in that they have been granted a higher degree of autonomy and lie outside the control of the local education authorities. However, 230 academies by 2010 will not be able to bridge the chasm that divides our education system. Roxburgh argued that the greatest opportunity for service offered to the private schools would be the assimilation of the brightest and best state educated pupils. We cannot afford to betray another generation by failing to make the most of our resources. The advantages currently enjoyed by children educated privately should be available to everyone without regard to wealth, status or background.

Only then will Britain be able to claim with any degree of legitimacy that it has a world-class system of education that serves all its people.

SUNDERLAND HIGH SCHOOL

'QUO VADIMUS?' (1937)

Edith M Ironside

Edith Ironside (can there be a more evocative name for a formidable Head Mistress of the 1930s?) writes of steering her school as a ship, led by the Spirit. She worries about the fierce criticism of institutional religion and of Christianity itself, and sees Churches emptying in spite of the thousands of young people being Confirmed in their faith each year: the fault must lie in a lack of guidance and support from both school and home. Education is concerned with 'the whole man, spiritual, intellectual and physical' – and 'all that can possibly be done for the last two, as this generation conceives it, is being done'.

But progress in education, and the 'increased standard of efficiency' has not made the world a better place:

We look out to-day upon such a medley of conduct and character as to make us wonder if we are entirely on wrong lines, seeing how soon, with shining exceptions, the individuality of the people we send out into the world seems to be allowing itself to be led blindly along, under at best questionable leadership.

Although Miss Ironside is less sure than many of her fellow contributors (a remarkably progressive bunch) about the new 'freedom' in schools, she shares with them (and surely with twenty-first century Head Teachers) a real worry about the 'cult of amusement', which is pushing aside 'simple pleasures' and 'the joy of anticipation':

> *Conversation, Music, Reading (not the imposter masquerading under its name) are banished by mechanized amusement: quiet evenings at home exist only for the very few. The idea of stewardship of money is out of date; the bewildering demands of fashion meet with an extraordinary response; mob psychology is amazing, the birth-rate disconcerting.*

Miss Ironside expresses concern about the new generation of teachers 'who a few years ago, were in someone else's VIth form'. They may be 'efficient, full of confidence, trained and alert', but they lack the 'background of culture .... true love of learning .... and the serenity that comes from an inner life of the spirit of .... older, less fashionable and somewhat haphazard colleagues'. For Miss Ironside, the teacher who combines the best of the old and the new is the ideal, 'but the moment the followers of the Profession tend to outnumber those of the Vocation, we shall be within measurable distance of shipwreck'.

Finally Miss Ironside points to the need for parents to play their part in education:

THE HEAD SPEAKS

Co-operation between the school and home is an overpowering necessity: so often loyalties are divided and the qualities, and actions and thoughts, on which the one – be it whichever it is – sets so high a value, are often treated by the other as of little account, so that utter bewilderment and lack of stability are the result....

The trouble is that the 'over-thirties' are so determined 'to respect personality' that they 'withhold the guidance that they are obviously in a position to give'.

A THREE-FOLD CHALLENGE

Angela Slater

No Headship interview is complete without an invitation to the candidate to deliver a vision for the school for the next ten years. The raw materials for that vision may amount to little more than a trawl through the school's website, a passing acquaintance with the accounts, and nuggets gleaned from obliging Sixth Formers during the guided tour. Small wonder that many Heads experience a shiver of embarrassment when they think back to that moment: the development of a vision takes both time and understanding. Suffice it to say that the degree of correlation between interview visions and outcomes achieved in post can be a fruitful area for research.

'The vision question', so easy to mock, is, of course, profoundly important. It is not enough for schools to exist for today, meeting the requirements of contemporary society: they must develop a vision for what lies ahead, a vision based upon an intelligent and creative assessment of the future in which their pupils will live and work. Much of what is happening in the educational world at the moment is driven by a recognition of that imperative. We are all busily building schools for the future, whether literally or metaphorically. If likely outcomes can be measured by bricks and column inches, that future is safe with us.

Or is it? What no one could have foreseen, even a few years ago, was the pace of change which would affect not only education but every area of contemporary life, sweeping away so many certainties in its wake. In 2006, Karl Fisch highlighted the daunting task facing the educational world in the context of a relentless chain of unknowns:

We are currently preparing students for jobs that don't yet exist, using technologies that haven't been invented, in order to solve problems we don't even know are problems yet.[1]

As an aside, even this daring rejection of certainties may prove to be conservative, for underpinning it is the assumption that a school's role in preparing pupils for employment will still be central in the future, an assumption some might regard as questionable. It reminds us yet again that however much we may try to think outside the box, we rarely escape its confines entirely.

Telling the future of education must start somewhere, however, and the view that new technological advances will be central to whatever happens is one to which most are happy to subscribe. Forget dry technical manuals – this will be a world of the unexpected and we must prepare accordingly:

Tomorrow's technology will always surprise us; we need

---

[1] These words are taken from a powerpoint presentation produced in August 2006 by Karl Fisch, a high school administrator at Arapahoe High School in Colorado. The presentation was entitled 'Did you know' and was initially intended for teachers at his school. It has since been viewed by millions worldwide.

buildings and systems that are ready for surprises! [2]

Most would agree that the first stage of the advance of new technology into schools has merely brought classrooms into the modern age. Pupils and teachers in the technology-starved classrooms of the 1990's were effectively operating on candlepower in a society which had long since invented electric light. They deserved to be able to access and exploit the sophisticated media to which they were accustomed at home. Interactive whiteboards, with all of the associated teaching and learning possibilities they bring, are now the norm in every school in the land. When their use is informed by all that we now know about how learning takes place, they enable teachers to respond in highly effective ways to the identified learning needs of small groups and individuals. When networked, they offer access to the infinite world of resources represented by the internet. It is not unusual to hear teachers who were already excellent practitioners say that they don't know how they ever managed without their 'board'.

The next stage in the advance of the electronic media is already well underway. As I write, each pupil in the country is aware of his or her entitlement to an e-portfolio. Schools are fine-tuning their Virtual Learning Environments. The educational world is looking at ways of harnessing the chameleon-like properties of mobile phone technology: is it a bird, is it a plane...? Other familiar routines are beginning to

---

[2] Professor Stephen Heppell, writing in *The Guardian* newspaper (p.10 of *Education Guardian*, 26.02.2008)

change. Thus, GCSE revision classes are as likely to take the form of a pod-cast – 'Instant access – anytime, anywhere!' – as that of the resigned end-of-day gathering of the faithful few who have reluctantly sacrificed football training for an extra hour in the classroom. School administration is being transformed by electronic registration and the resultant automatically triggered text messages to the unwitting parents of absent pupils.

Happy to heed the siren call of the electronic media, schools have as yet remained relatively conservative when it comes to the transformation of teaching spaces. Heppel's optimistic call for 'buildings ... that are ready for surprises' seems to have fallen largely on deaf ears. Building materials may have changed; and there have undoubtedly been superficial changes to accommodate the new technology referred to above; but, these things apart, the majority of classrooms would still be all too familiar to those teaching decades ago. This more than anything else suggests just how uncertain schools are about their role in the future: it's difficult to change if you are unsure what you are changing for.

The challenge facing schools in this respect is mirrored in the challenge for churches around the country, where 're-ordering' is currently the order of the day. Our own parish church, for example, which has existed for at least nine hundred years, is currently fundraising to support its campaign for 'the next 900'. Nothing like an ambitious development programme: for most schools, 'the next twenty' would do. Is there anything for us to learn from the churches in all of this?

First impressions might suggest not. From the outside and to the determinedly cynical, church re-ordering can seem nothing more than the decision to jettison fixed pews in favour of moveable chairs, instal a carefully screened digital projector and open a coffee shop. (The school equivalents are not hard to find.) To stop there, however, would be to miss the point: the driving force behind church re-ordering is the probing and soul-searching which may or may not generate such developments. What is the mission of a church? Do church practices need to change to reflect that mission? Do church buildings need to change to facilitate those new practices? As with churches, so with schools, the greatest challenge is, surely, to redefine the mission. Once that is done, it is a relatively simple process of amending practices and adapting facilities, under the watchful eye of a good project manager.

What, then, is a school's mission? My own view is that schools have a three-fold challenge. First, to equip pupils with the skills set to exploit, rather than be exploited by, the explosion in information represented by the world wide web. Second, to nurture in pupils the values and sound judgment required by citizens of 'cyberia'[3] if they are to emerge unscathed from their teenage dalliance with this emerging empire, situated at the interface between humans and computers. Third, to expose pupils to a range of experiences and challenges which will engender in them the qualities that characterize outstanding individuals.

---

[3] This evocative word is cited by Ivana Milojevic in *Educational Futures. Dominant and Contesting Visions,* New York: Routledge (2005). It seems to have been coined in 1996: see Sardar, Z. *Cyberfutures: Culture and Politics on the Information Superhighway,* New York: New York University Press (1996).

The first two will facilitate the successful navigation of situations which already exist, albeit in embryonic form, and which will surely continue to expand and mutate, to the despair of the old and the bring-it-on delight of the young. The third will enable pupils to plot a route through territory as yet totally uncharted, indeed, not even discovered. Those who possess this portfolio of skills, values and personal qualities will be positioned to meet the challenges of the future in a way of which the present-day recipients of a sheaf of traditional examination certificates can only dream.

Let's take the challenge of technology first, in the form of the exponential growth in the amount of information 'out there', courtesy of the electronic media. 'Infoglut'[4] is one particularly effective word which has been coined to describe this phenomenon. The excitement which initially greeted a school's ability instantly to expand the learning resources available to its pupils to the nth degree by installing broadband and allowing access to a range of carefully vetted websites has in some quarters given way to despair as the information floodgates have opened. Where does a pupil start to make sense of it all?

Search engines help, of course, but they do not provide a quality rating: paradoxically, the quality assurance mechanisms by which the educational world rightly sets such store are rarely to be seen in what is one of the most powerful forces for change in that same world. Further, the experience-based selection criteria which assist an adult surfer to know which web pages to trust are by definition rarely

---

[4] Milojevic, I. (2005) p. 102

present in the mind of a child. It is up to schools, therefore, to equip their pupils to operate successfully in this limitless minefield of information.

Pupils must be taught, from a very early age, not only how to search for information – the easy bit – but how to evaluate that information when they have found it. They need discernment and discretion. They must understand what leads people to write, and what authors hope to achieve by their writing. They must learn to recognize bias and prejudice. They must develop the skills of selection, collation and synthesis. These are the skills of the English classroom. They are the skills of the history classroom. They are the skills of the laboratory and of the debating chamber. So far, so familiar. Except that these skills must move centre-stage: they are essential to educational health and survival. When they have acquired this particular skills set, pupils will be able fully to benefit from the most wonderful, infinitely expanding world of information. And they will still be in control.

There will be some who feel that all this is beginning to sound rather too serious. Why all the panic? Isn't technology just a tool? Isn't this simply a case of middle-aged school leaders realizing that they will only ever be several steps behind their pupils, and over-reacting accordingly?

There may well be an element of that, of course, and most schools would do well to retain a sense of humour in the face of what can seem an unstoppable tide of variations upon the electronic theme. The on-going saga of the school mobile telephone policy provides a cautionary tale in this respect.

It was a relatively simple thing for schools to develop a mobile telephone policy when phones were phones. It wasn't too difficult to amend it when phones became cameras. When, at a particular moment in time, the number of phones going off during Assembly throughout the land plummeted, Heads joyfully attributed the fall to the effectiveness of the aforementioned policy. It was some time before they realized that this had happened simply because those same phones were now on 'vibrate'. Even that technological development seems simple to deal with, however, when faced with a generation of phones whose ring tone is deliberately set outside the hearing frequency range of the average adult. Wry smiles all round as we try to work out a solution to that one.

Where it is difficult for a school to retain a sense of humour is in the face of the average teenager's inability to negotiate the many social and emotional pitfalls inherent in the new technologies. Indeed, experience of the way in which pastoral care is beginning to be dominated by the virtual world suggests that a sense of despair might be more appropriate. We may remind ourselves that communication is a good thing, and that the wonders of the electronic media provide incredible opportunities to strengthen and develop friendships. We may warm to the thrill of linking up with a school in Africa, an adventure which brings untold benefits, opening up young hearts and minds. We are painfully aware, however, that each new mutation of the electronic media brings so many more traps for the unsuspecting teenager to fall into, and that relatively few manage to steer clear entirely.

The pitfalls may take the form of the hours spent each evening engaged in instant messaging, utilizing the brutal, ugly language which seems to be *de rigueur* for that activity. Or the creation of an indiscreet social profile, 'just for a laugh', with little thought for the consequences, either immediate or several years down the line – for whenever did teenagers think of consequences? Or the posting of unkind or unwise messages, instantly available to be forwarded to a multiplicity of other individuals and impossible to retrieve. And all this, of course, safe in the illusion that somehow it doesn't really matter: the virtual world is another country, they do things differently there. Nothing counts. Until, that is, a crumpled print-out of an electronic 'conversation' is shamefacedly handed to parents by the modern-day victim of cyberbullying who can't take any more, at which point we are back on more familiar pastoral territory.

What is needed here is more than just a few lessons of Personal and Social Education, typically delivered by a non-specialist and frequently sacrificed to whatever more pressing event is going on in school at the time. Young people need a survival package. They need access to a carefully constructed, expertly delivered, cyclical programme of activities, discussions and events which will both introduce them to and nurture in them the personal qualities required to navigate the social and emotional challenges which the new technologies bring, and compared with which traditional pastoral concerns can seem child's play. What is more, they need to see these qualities modelled by the adults around them: an enormous responsibility by any standard. Schools in the electronic age must move this life-critical guidance centre-stage: it is far too important to be confined to the wings.

Whatever the challenges presented by the electronic media,

whether in their current or their future manifestations, they at least have the virtue of existing: we know something of our opponent. Clearly, the same cannot be said for the third dimension of a school's challenge, and this makes the task so much more daunting. Precisely because the future is unknowable, schools must prepare their pupils to cope with the possibility of constant change. They can only do this by developing and nurturing in them the qualities and aptitudes which will fit them for, and enable them to flourish in, any set of circumstances. What, then, are these qualities and aptitudes? Let's pay a call to the recent gathering of the Society of Heads of Independent Schools, where this year's conference theme was 'Good to great'. Two of the keynote speakers addressed questions which have more than a passing relevance to our discussion.

The Chief Inspector at the Independent Schools Inspectorate was invited to identify the characteristics of a great school. Her challenging answer included a reference to the qualities which would be displayed by the pupils of such a school. Among the qualities discussed were curiosity, confidence, tolerance, resourcefulness, adaptability and a willingness to take risks. The development of these qualities in pupils requires high quality teachers, we were reminded, teachers who plan for learning rather than for teaching.

At the same gathering, a university vice chancellor talked about the creation of great graduates. He spoke proudly of the way in which his university's undergraduates took every opportunity to engage in the community, whether at a local, national or global level. He reflected upon what schools could do to assist universities in their mission. Without hesitation, he declared that we must teach beyond the syllabus. In other words, whether at a community or an academic level, we must encourage our young people to think and act beyond what is strictly necessary.

These answers were not directed specifically towards future needs, but together they identify some of the qualities, attitudes and opportunities which are likely to enable young people to feel properly equipped as they peer into an uncertain future. The good news is that this dimension of future-proofing is already fully embedded in school life. It is found in the classrooms of teachers whose passion for their subject combines with a profound commitment to the development of their pupils to create an environment of mutual trust, where it is acceptable to take risks, fly kites and leave the security of the scheme of work. It characterizes the myriad of opportunities unceremoniously grouped together under the title of extra-curricular provision, and ranging from the adrenalin rush of the opening night of the school play to the dripping tents of the Duke of Edinburgh practice expedition. It is the rationale behind the pupil voice; and it is the reason why it is sometimes important to allow pupil-driven initiatives to fail, so that next time – re-thought, re-designed and re-presented – they meet with success.

The challenge for schools is to allow all of these elements to come in out of the cold, to afford them a position of centrality rather than trying to fit them in around the edges. If we truly believe that the qualities and aptitudes engendered by enrichment programmes are central to our mission, then we must have the courage of our convictions and grant them the prominence and influence their new status merits. This does not necessarily signal the end of the curriculum as we know it, but it does mean that the way that curriculum is delivered will consciously facilitate and encourage the development of the qualities we have been discussing.

In the end, therefore, whether we are talking about infoglut, cyberia or the sheer unknowability of what lies ahead, the challenge for schools is one and the same: to strive to develop in the young people entrusted to them the skills and qualities which will enable them not merely to cope but to flourish in the situations we have considered. All of the resources at a school's disposal – the teachers, the curriculum, the buildings, the time – must be treated not as separate empires, not as ends in themselves, but as functions of this greater goal. If the future is indeed to be safe with us, this is the standard against which everything that happens in a school must be measured.

Other Books from the University of Buckingham Press

Can the Prizes Still Glitter?
The Future of British Universities in a Changing World
ISBN 095546420X RRP £15.99
Edited by Hugo de Burgh, Anna Fazackerley and Jeremy Black

"This is a timely and provocative book addressing some of the key challenges facing the HE sector in a series of papers by the leaders and innovators in the field." Dame Nancy Rothwell FRS, Vice President and MRC Research Professor, The University of Manchester.

Contributors include: Sir Harry Kroto, David Palfreyman, Bernard Lamb, Kenneth Minogue, Boris Johnson, Bill Rammell, Terence Kealey, Alex Reed and other leading authorities in the HE field.

Inside the Secret Garden
The Progressive Decay of Liberal Education
ISBN 0955464218 RRP £12.99

Tom Burkard, Foreword by Dennis O'Keeffe

Despite unprecedented increases in education spending, standards are plummeting, and at least 20% of our children can't even read. Tom Burkard shows how an intellectually misguided elite - claiming to be experts in child development and psychology - have subverted the will of the people and used our children as guinea pigs in a grand 'experiment' that has gone horribly wrong.

Tom Burkard highlights the central paradox of progressive education - that despite the professed aim of creating a more democratic society it would be almost impossible to design a system better suited to perpetrating both class divisions and the gulf between the have and have-nots